T0323907

Cambridge Elements ≡

Elements in Publishing and Book Culture
edited by
Samantha Rayner
University College London
Leah Tether
University of Bristol

BEHAVIOUR BEYOND THE TEXT AND THE MORALITY CLAUSE IN TWENTY-FIRST-CENTURY PUBLISHING

Chiara Bullen
University of Stirling

CAMBRIDGE
UNIVERSITY PRESS

Shaftesbury Road, Cambridge CB2 8EA, United Kingdom

One Liberty Plaza, 20th Floor, New York, NY 10006, USA

477 Williamstown Road, Port Melbourne, VIC 3207, Australia

314–321, 3rd Floor, Plot 3, Splendor Forum, Jasola District Centre,
New Delhi – 110025, India

103 Penang Road, #05–06/07, Visioncrest Commercial, Singapore 238467

Cambridge University Press is part of Cambridge University Press & Assessment,
a department of the University of Cambridge.

We share the University's mission to contribute to society through the pursuit of
education, learning and research at the highest international levels of excellence.

www.cambridge.org
Information on this title: www.cambridge.org/9781009573177

DOI: 10.1017/9781009573184

© Chiara Bullen 2024

This publication is in copyright. Subject to statutory exception and to the provisions
of relevant collective licensing agreements, no reproduction of any part may take
place without the written permission of Cambridge University Press & Assessment.

When citing this work, please include a reference to the DOI 10.1017/9781009573184

First published 2024

A catalogue record for this publication is available from the British Library.

ISBN 978-1-009-57317-7 Paperback
ISSN 2514-8524 (online)
ISSN 2514-8516 (print)

Cambridge University Press & Assessment has no responsibility for the persistence
or accuracy of URLs for external or third-party internet websites referred to in this
publication and does not guarantee that any content on such websites is, or will
remain, accurate or appropriate.

Behaviour Beyond the Text
and the Morality Clause
in Twenty-First-Century Publishing

Elements in Publishing and Book Culture

DOI: 10.1017/9781009573184
First published online: December 2024

Chiara Bullen
University of Stirling

Author for correspondence: Chiara Bullen, chiara.bullen@stir.ac.uk

ABSTRACT: A morality clause allows contracting parties to terminate a contractual agreement with those who exhibit behaviour deemed unacceptable. Established in 1920s Hollywood, these contractual clauses are now found in twenty-first-century publishing agreements. This Element investigates the presence of the morality clause in the UK book publishing industry in relation to an increased focus on author behaviour beyond the text in the twenty-first century, examining the way it operates within the publishing field in the context of behaviour perceived to be 'problematic'. It asserts the clause is perceived to be needed due to the emergence of social media and twenty-first-century social contexts combining to impact the author–reader relationship which, in turn, leads to author behaviour acting as a paratextual threshold to their work. This Element presents an analysis of the morality clause in practice, concluding that the clause has the potential to further the power imbalance between author and publisher.

KEYWORDS: morality clause, twenty-first-century authorship, book publishing, author–reader relationship, literature

© Chiara Bullen 2024

ISBNs: 9781009573177 (PB), 9781009573184 (OC)
ISSNs: 2514-8524 (online), 2514-8516 (print)

Contents

1 Introduction

In 2016, 'alt-right' journalist Milo Yiannopoulos was offered a book deal.[1] 'I met with top execs at Simon & Schuster earlier in the year and spent half an hour trying to shock them with lewd jokes and outrageous opinions', Yiannopoulos told *The Hollywood Reporter* on announcing the deal. 'I thought they were going to have me escorted from the building – but instead they offered me a wheelbarrow full of money' (Bond 2016). The 'wheelbarrow full of money' reportedly took the form of a $250,000 advance (Bond 2016). However, some readers and other agents in the publishing field opposed Yiannopoulos being given a 'serious' platform to express his views (Phillips 2019, 158). In the wake of the book deal, *The Chicago Review of Books* announced on Twitter they would not offer review space for any forthcoming Simon & Schuster titles, arguing the deal was a 'disgusting validation of hate' (Grady 2017, Stefansky 2016). Some authors expressed hesitancy at continuing their working relationship with Simon & Schuster (Jamieson 2017), an independent bookstore stated they would no longer stock Simon & Schuster titles, and some readers exclaimed on social media they could not support a publisher who platformed the author (Fallon 2016).

The publishing field experienced disruption in the wake of this incident, with members of the industry in conflict about whether or not Yiannopoulos being offered a book deal was acceptable conduct on the part of Simon & Schuster. In early 2017, Simon & Schuster terminated Yiannopoulos' contract, citing that the manuscript was not of the quality they established in the terms of the publishing agreement (Phillips 2019, 158). Nevertheless, speculation within the industry followed about why the publishing agreement was terminated, as Yiannopoulos' termination came shortly after he made comments accused to be endorsing 'child abuse' (Malkin and Jacobs 2017) which

---

[1] Alt-right is short for 'alternative right', and alt-right views are defined as 'an ideological grouping associated with extreme conservative or reactionary viewpoints, characterized by a rejection of mainstream politics and by the use of online media to disseminate deliberately controversial content' (Schuessler 2016). Yiannopoulos is often described as 'alt-right' in the media (see, for example, BBC News 2017).

incited further criticism of the author and Simon & Schuster (Deahl 2018). Yiannopoulos summoned Simon & Schuster to court over the termination, expressing the belief that his views beyond the text, as opposed to the quality of the manuscript, were the reason for termination. The court summons, accessible online, states: 'Simon & Schuster wrongfully, and in bad faith, terminated the contract with Yiannopoulos in violation of its terms and cancelled *Dangerous* under pressure from authors, bookselling accounts, business and special-interest groups, celebrities, and various other self-appointed censors who disagreed with views expressed by Yiannopoulos.'[2]

With Simon & Schuster citing the quality of the manuscript as the reason for the termination (and, due to the publicised court documentation, the manuscript draft along with the editorial comments are available online for readers to draw their own conclusions on this matter (Belam 2017)), it cannot be conclusively said that Yiannopoulos' behaviour contributed to the contract's termination.[3] Nevertheless, the Yiannopoulos incident sparked widespread discussions about whether an author's behaviour beyond the text should or should not affect their publishing career (Deahl 2018, Shulevitz 2019).

Publishers acting to distance themselves from authors displaying problematic behaviours and opinions has become increasingly apparent across the US and UK book publishing industries in the twenty-first century. The term 'problematic' can be used to describe those who 'are assessed to have said or done something unacceptable ... generally from a social justice perspective especially alert to sexism, heterosexism, homophobia, racism, bullying, and related issues' (Ng 2020, 623). Schmitz (2015) states that the word 'problematic' is 'one of the indispensable words of our time, a catch-all for any ... misstep or media mishap that could [have] sexist, racist, or hegemonic implications'. The term was brought into popularity by the 'Your Fave is

---

[2] *Milo Yiannopoulous* v. *Simon & Schuster Inc*, New York County Court, 7 July 2017. www.courthousenews.com/wp-content/uploads/2017/07/milo-yiannopoulos .pdf.

[3] While no morality clause is present in Milo Yiannopoulos' contract issued in 2016, Somers (2018), reporting for *Publishers' Lunch*, asserts the presence of a morality clause in some Simon & Schuster contracts in 2018.

Problematic' blog founded in 2010 (Clayman Pye 2022, 167),[4] a blog that, in the words of its founder, 'contained long lists of celebrities' regrettable (racist, sexist, homophobic, transphobic, ethnophobic, ableist and so on) statements and actions – the stuff that gets people canceled' (Kaplan 2021). Sánchez Abril and Greene (2017) observe the need for 'associates' to distance themselves from individuals associated with such behaviour across industries: 'In a society in which insensitivity and intolerance are the subjects of widespread public shaming … Associates of the politically incorrect often receive immense pressure to denounce the questionable behavior, or risk being perceived as condoning it' (24).

Such 'public shaming' often occurs on social media (and, in the case of publishing, via reader review sites such as Goodreads), meaning criticisms of and accusations towards authors can be seen publicly, often before being picked up by the media. Sánchez Abril and Greene's observation that organisations can be seen as 'condoning' behaviour suggests that publishers could also be viewed as 'condoning' the behaviours and views exhibited by their authors. Indeed, this notion was apparently felt by Simon & Schuster before they decided to terminate Milo Yiannopoulos' memoir, officially stating they have never 'condoned discrimination or hate speech', and instead sought to publish 'authors with greatly varying, and frequently controversial opinions' (Stefansky 2016).

One practice has emerged across industries to allow contracting parties to exit agreements with contracted individuals should they behave in a way the contracting party deem to be 'reprehensible': the morality clause (Pinguelo and Cedrone 2009, 358, 351). The definition of 'morality clause' can and does differ from contract to contract. For the purposes of this Element, the definition put forward by Pinguelo and Cedrone in their seminal discussion on the morality clause is appropriate:

> [A morality clause] is a contractual provision that gives one
> contracting party (usually a company) the unilateral right to
> terminate the agreement, or take punitive action against the

---

[4] At the time of writing in 2023, the blog has been inactive for approximately seven years.

> other party in the event that such other party engages in
> reprehensible behaviour or conduct that may negatively
> impact his or her public image and, by association, the public
> image of the contracting company. (351)

The morality clause has appeared in publishing agreements across the US
and the UK throughout the twenty-first century, from Random House
Children's Books in the early 2000s in the UK (Jones 2008), HarperCollins
US in 2010 (Novelists Inc. 2010), and Simon & Schuster and Penguin
Random House in 2018 (Somers 2018). This Element is an investigation of
the emergence of the morality clause in the book publishing industry, as
well as the increased focus on author behaviour beyond the text more
generally in the twenty-first century. It asks: why has the morality clause
emerged in publishing agreements, and what impact does its presence
have on agents in the publishing field? This Element ultimately presents
the argument that the changing author–reader relationship (driven by
advances in social media alongside twenty-first-century social contexts)
means that an author's behaviour beyond the text is more visible than ever
and can act as a paratextual threshold to their work. This, in turn, has
created a perceived need for the morality clause in publishing agreements
as the life of the author beyond the text can negatively impact associated
publisher reputation and finances should audiences demonstrate widescale
disapproval of an author's behaviour. Such a dynamic is, I argue, indicative of a changing habitus as experienced by authors, editors, and literary
agents in the publishing field, the morality clause's presence and the
increased focus on authors' behaviour beyond the text placing new
expectations on authorship in the twenty-first century.

1.1 Key Incidents: Author Behaviour beyond the Text

This section presents 'key incidents' that illustrate objections to perceived
problematic behaviour across the US and UK publishing industries. I have
deemed the following examples 'key incidents' due to the attention they
received; namely, media and trade publication coverage due to, for instance,
a mass negative reaction from audiences. This section does not comprise
a comprehensive list; instead, it gives a brief account of selected incidents to

contextualise later analysis of problematic behaviour and the emergence of the morality clause in the publishing field.

High-profile progressive social movements have created a renewed, heightened awareness of social inequalities across the creative industries (Ali 2023, Brook et al. 2020, chap. 9). In late 2017, Tarana Burke's #MeToo movement rose to prominence, and the world grappled with instances of sexual abuse, assault, harassment, and injustice that were often otherwise brushed under the rug (Williams et al. 2019, 374). Perhaps most publicised is the movement's impact in Hollywood, which subsequently sparked the revival of the morality clause in the film industry (Sheikha 2019). A similar disruption occurred within the publishing field, with authors losing their positions throughout the height of the #MeToo movement. For example, online news publication *Vox* curated a list of individuals in the media industry (amongst others) accused of sexual assault, abuse, or harassment (North 2017). Authors Junot Díaz and Sherman Alexie are named on the list (North 2017). Junot Díaz stepped down as chairman of the Pulitzer Prize after harassment accusations (he was reinstated after an independent review; Flood 2018a), while The Institute of American Indian Arts revoked a scholarship in Alexie's name following harassment allegations (Bullen 2022, Flood 2018b). Outside of the *Vox* list, in 2021 W. W. Norton halted the publication of Blake Bailey's Phillip Roth biography in the US after Bailey faced multiple sexual assault allegations (Anthony 2021). The title was later published by Skyhorse Publishing and by Vintage UK (Anthony 2021). The initial action taken against these figures – and many others – suggests an awareness from book publishers and creative organisations that some audiences demonstrate a lack of tolerance for problematic behaviour associated with the #MeToo movement. Each author listed here has, in various ways, acted to reposition themselves in the field, but this does not change the fact that the combining forces of the #MeToo movement and pressure from audiences altered their position in the first place. In these examples, whether the morality clause was used or not is unclear – although some reports suggest that Bailey's contract was terminated in this way (Clark 2022). Alter (2018), observing the impact of the #MeToo movement in the US publishing industry, states: 'As allegations of sexual harassment sweep through the publishing industry – resulting in canceled book deals, boycotts by bookstores and expulsions from writers' conferences – publishers, agents and editors are grappling with how to tackle the issue … publishing and promoting a book by an author accused of misconduct can have other negative ramifications.' Lipton (2020) makes a similar observation: 'In the age of the #MeToo movement, several authors have found their agents or editors cutting ties with them because they don't want to be associated with authors who have, or are getting, a bad reputation in the industry' (118).

As discussed previously, the incident with Milo Yiannopoulos highlighted an instance of behaviour beyond the text leading to audience objections ahead of publication. Another case of an author's behaviour beyond the text leading to objections prior to publication is that of Julie Burchill and Little, Brown. In this case, the behaviour was linked to the decision from the publisher, with Little, Brown stating that Burchill's 'Islamophobic' (Bland 2021) comments were 'not defensible from a moral or intellectual standpoint' when announcing the termination of the contract (Nugent 2020). J. K. Rowling has also faced criticisms for being 'problematic' (Romano 2020). Rowling's social media posts and written work expressing her views about transgender women caused a split amongst her fans (Velasco 2020, 4), with some readers stating they would boycott Rowling's work as a result (Chilton 2020).

Publishing staff have also expressed objections to perceived problematic behaviour exhibited by authors. Protests from publisher employees occurred in 2020 and 2021, including staff at Hachette US protesting the publication of a memoir from Woody Allen due to the sexual assault allegations made against him (Williams 2020), staff at Hachette UK threatening to walk out over the publishing of J. K. Rowling's 2020 title in the wake of her comments regarding transgender women (Cowdrey 2020), and staff at Penguin Random House Canada protesting the continued publication of psychologist Jordan Peterson (Flood 2020b).

As highlighted by these key incidents, perceived problematic behaviours demonstrated by authors outside of their publications are something that audiences have been particularly attuned to in the 2010s and 2020s. The many key incidents from 2010 onwards, as well as the progressive social movements that emerged in the 2010s, led me to establish the timeframe of this Element; its analysis specifically captures the years 2010–21. The year

2010 also coincides with the rapid development of social media's role in the publishing industry (see Chapter 2) and saw one of the earliest morality clauses in the publishing industry being contested (see Chapters 3 and 4).

1.2 A History of the Morality Clause: From 1920s Hollywood to Twenty-First-Century Book Publishing

Looking at early uses of the morality clause across creative industries presents insights into its use in the twenty-first-century publishing industry, as some of the present-day concerns surrounding morality clause usage have been present since its inception in the twentieth century.

In 1921, silent film-star Roscoe 'Fatty' Arbuckle was arrested on charges of sexual assault and murder after signing a multi-million-dollar contract for future productions with Paramount Pictures (*New York Times* 1921, 8). In response, Universal Studios inserted a morality clause in contracts for actors in their employ, hoping to avoid the financial and reputational repercussions Paramount Pictures faced. As reported by the *New York Times*, this first morality clause in the film industry reads as follows:

> The actor (actress) agrees to conduct himself (herself) with due regard to public conventions and morals and agrees that he (she) will not do or commit anything tending to degrade him (her) in society or bring him (her) into public hatred, contempt, scorn or ridicule, or tending to shock, insult or offend the community or outrage public morals or decency, or rending to the prejudice of the Universal Film Manufacturing company or the motion picture industry. In the event that the actor (actress) violates any term or provision of this paragraph, then the Universal Film Manufacturing company has the right to cancel and annul this contract by giving five (5) days' notice to the actor (actress) of its intention to do so. (*New York Times* 1921, 8)

Cooley et al. (2008) observe that during the early twentieth century there existed an 'intense public scrutiny of morality within the motion picture industry' (3), triggered by scandals such as Arbuckle's. Gallagher (2016) also notes that during the early twentieth century it was 'hypothesized that film ticket sales had declined because of the perception that "stars" were leading "sinful, off-screen lives"' (93). Such an observation implies that audiences have long demonstrated their potential power as a consumer when an artist displays behaviour they disapprove of, paralleling the situation Sánchez Abril and Greene (2017) outline in the twenty-first century, highlighting the 'scrutiny' and 'public shaming' that are suffered by organisations associated with individuals exhibiting problematic behaviour (24). The terms included in the Universal Studios morality clause such as 'public hatred' and 'contempt' (*New York Times* 1921, 8) could refer to a wide number of behaviours that may potentially provoke negative public responses, none of which are made clear or defined. Such vagueness or ambiguity of the morality clause is addressed in scholarly work on the clause across entertainment industries (Epstein 2015, Katz 2011, Kressler 2005, Pinguelo and Cedrone 2009, Sánchez Abril and Greene 2017, Sheikha 2019). As is acknowledged by Pinguelo and Cedrone (2009), there is often a power imbalance between the contracted talent and the contracting company, with the latter typically inclined to include wide-reaching, ambiguous morality clauses in order to offer themselves the most 'protection' (352).

In 1931, actress and singer Mary Lewis attempted to sue Pathé Company for breach of contract after they cancelled her upcoming films (Dougan 1977, 275). Pathé responded that they terminated her contract due to Lewis violating the morality clause in her contractual agreement. Pathé claimed Lewis '[became] intoxicated and involved in a scandal, and became the subject of comment by publications' (Dougan 1977, 275, *New York Times* 1931, 26). Dougan (2018) highlights the ambiguity regarding Lewis' alleged behaviour and the economic crisis facing the film industry at the time:

> As the Depression deepened and audiences thinned, the movie industry was in crisis due to too many musical 'talkie' films. Lewis's films were cancelled, and Mary sued for breach of contract. Pathé claimed she had violated the 'morals clause' and cited some unspecified incident. One known episode was when she collapsed or was hauled off the stage during

a Sunday evening national radio show ... Lewis further
suffered from the repercussions of her divorce. (282)

The Lewis case highlights two objections still present against morality clause
usage in the twenty-first century, particularly across the entertainment industries. Pathé may have cited the morality clause as the reason for termination,
yet the cancellation of the films Lewis was due to star in came during a time of
industry struggle (Dougan 2018, 282). The possibility of abuse of power from
organisations attempting to retain profits by citing the morality clause as the
reason for termination when the decision is in fact driven by financial motiva-
tion is a worry present across industries today. As Sánchez Abril and Greene
(2017) argue, 'If employers and other contracting parties are given unlimited
discretion to interpret broad, all-encompassing morals clauses, they could
quite easily use these clauses to terminate an economically disappointing
relationship under the pretence of moral objection' (42).

In 2018, one literary agent speaking to *Publishers Weekly* expressed
a similar concern about the morality clause: 'Maybe [the publisher] signs
up three books for $1 million, and the first book doesn't do so well, and
they use this clause to get around what's legal and fair' (Deahl 2018).
While this hypothetical scenario is one that in reality may be difficult to
prove should it reach the courtroom, it highlights an overarching 'fear' of
the morality clause, echoed in interviews for this Element (see Chapter 3).
As Lipton (2020) notes: 'It can be difficult for an author to prove that the
publisher actually cancelled a contract because of morality concerns rather
than concerns about satisfactory writing' (118). The Lewis case also
highlights the ever-changing definitions of what constitutes good 'moral
behaviour', as well as the wide scope of the clause – even if Pathé did
indeed terminate the agreement due to her behaviour, her actions are
a world away from Arbuckle's alleged actions that triggered morality
clause usage in Hollywood ten years prior. The difference in moral
standards expected of men and women in the industry at this time may
well have had an impact on what behaviour would trigger a clause for
Lewis but perhaps not for a male colleague. Lewis' case highlights the
significance of social contexts when examining the use of the morality
clause in any given industry.

Morality clause use continued throughout the twentieth century (see, for example, Epstein's (2015) discussion of the 'Hollywood Ten' and the morality clause (76)), and its use particularly increased within 'talent contracts' (Pinguelo and Cedrone 2009, 356). Osborn Hill (2010) summarises an organisation's perceived need for a morality clause when working with celebrities in the context of endorsement contracts: 'The hope is that the public will become comfortable with the product because they are comfortable with the celebrity spokesperson. However ... when the celebrity starts behaving in a way that is likely to offend the purchasing public, the negative public perception may also be transferred to the product' (14). The 'transference' of public perception from the 'celebrity' to the 'product' is similar to the author and the publisher brand being closely associated (Gardiner 2000, 67), as discussed in Chapters 2 and 3. The morality clause then became a point of focus in Hollywood in the twenty-first century. Acknowledging the #MeToo movement's impact on the film industry from 2017 onwards, Sheikha (2019) observes that 'A mere social media hashtag [#MeToo] instilled fear into the hearts of prominent male celebrities ... The upper echelon of Hollywood took notice and scrambled for a means to distance themselves from toxic talent and terminate their existing contracts' (204).

In the immediate wake of the #MeToo movement, hundreds of individuals lost 'powerful' positions due to alleged sexual misconduct (Carlsen et al. 2018), and scholars such as Morris (2019) have advised organisations in the US to utilise 'morals clauses' due to the impact of the #MeToo movement (46).

Much scholarly work on the morality clause revolves around its historic and post-#MeToo inclusion in the film industries (Davidson 2020, Gallagher 2016, Sheikha 2019), sport contracts (J. Murray 2018, Zarriello 2015), and within the wider entertainment and creative industries – such as TV personality, endorsement, and fashion contracts (Kressler 2005, Pinguelo and Cedrone 2009). These works also place particular emphasis on the clause's presence in the United States, where it is more widely used. A study that fleetingly mentions the use of the morality clause in UK publishing is that of Pinguelo and Cedrone (2009, 365), alluding to the clause being introduced in UK publishing in the early 2000s via Random House Children's Books (Jones 2008). Other uses of the clause in the publishing industry include HarperCollins US in 2010 (Novelists Inc. 2010), and Simon & Schuster, HarperCollins, and Penguin Random House US in 2018 (Somers 2018). Koegler et al. (2023) examine how morality clauses used in US publishing agreements would stand in the context of German civil law, and posit that the clause is 'permitted within certain limits in individually negotiated contracts'. This Element takes a similar approach to Koegler et al. in that it explores the clause's effectiveness within a legal jurisdiction (in this case, England and Wales) alongside an interrogation into its emergence and impact in the UK publishing field.

1.3 Theoretical Framework

This Element examines the morality clause in the publishing industry, applying Bourdieu's theories of the field, capital, and habitus, and later draws on Genette's theory of paratext to highlight the importance placed on an author's behaviour beyond the text in the twenty-first century.

The field, as depicted by Bourdieu, is the space agents and their social positions occupy. Agents include publishing staff, reviewers, authors, publishing houses themselves as entities, and literary agents. As Bourdieu (1993) explains, 'The literary field (one may also speak of the artistic field, the philosophical field, etc.) is an independent social universe with its own laws of functioning, its specific relations of force ... to speak of 'field' is to recall that literary works are produced in a particular social universe endowed with particular institutions and obeying specific laws' (163). Bourdieu also argues that the field 'functions somewhat like a prism which refracts every external determination', observing that economic and political events are 'retranslated' due to the 'specific' logic of the field (1993, 164). The habitus, as described by Bourdieu (1990), is 'a system of cognitive and motivating structures, [it] is a world of already realized ends – procedures to follow, paths to take' (53). Ungure (2020) and Gūtmane identify habitus as following the 'rules of the game' within a particular field, reliant on an agent's social position within it (36). Gulledge et al. (2015) elaborate that habitus is the 'ability to master what is required to function' within the field (642), and is what Bourdieu (1998) also refers to as the 'feel for the game' which is 'turned into second nature' (25; Gulledge et al. 2015, 650). Like Gulledge et al. (2015), I refer to the 'specific' habitus of agents: 'the habitus of the "priest, journalist, doctor, boxer, scientist" [is] the development of dispositions "to be and to do" as a priest, journalist, doctor, boxer or scientist, where a specific habitus incorporates the particular logic of the field' (639). I assert that whether a morality clause is inserted into a publishing agreement or not, instances of authors losing contracts or other positions in the publishing field suggests a changing habitus and changing notions of what is considered, in Gulledge's (2011) terms, 'unreasonable' conduct within the publishing field (44). Writing in 2018, the editor of UK trade magazine *The Bookseller* acknowledged this change: 'We cannot pretend that the atmosphere for writers hasn't shifted. Social media brings with it a new way of policing authors, and their words, that publishers should resist, not prep lawyers to use' (Jones 2018). While Jones seemingly rejects the emergence of the morality clause by acknowledging the 'prepping' of lawyers, Jones' comments imply that the 'rules of the game' (Ungure and Gūtmane 2020, 36) have 'shifted' for agents navigating the publishing field. The position of each agent in the field is dependent on the interaction between specific rules of the field and the agent's accumulated capital: 'Economic capital, which is immediately and directly convertible into money … cultural capital, which is convertible, in certain conditions, into economic capital … and … social capital, made up of social obligations ('connections'), which is convertible, in certain conditions, into economic capital' (Bourdieu 1986, 242).

There also exists symbolic capital, which Thompson (2012) states 'is best understood as the accumulated prestige, recognition and respect accorded to certain individuals or institutions' (6), and which Lebaron notes is accumulated through 'acting in conformity with the rules of the field' (Lebaron 2014, 6539). Habitus, capital, and the field are interdependent, as demonstrated by Bourdieu's (2010) formula: [(habitus)(capital)] + field = practice (95).

Genette's (1997) theory of paratext is also useful to consider when investigating the increased focus on author behaviour beyond the text. Paratext is a 'threshold' to the text, offering the opportunity to step 'inside' or '[turn] back' from a book (2). Paratext primarily consists of two concepts: the peritext (elements that make up and/or are within a book, such as title, cover, etc.) and the epitext, which is typically a 'spatial' aspect that manifests beyond and around the text (3). For instance, author interviews and marketing content for the book are considered epitext. This Element argues that an author's life beyond the text – their behaviours, their views – can act as epitextual elements of their texts in the twenty-first century. The aforementioned incident concerning Milo Yiannopoulos serves as an example here: the behaviour of Yiannopoulos acted as an epitextual threshold to his work *Dangerous* prior to its intended publication, apparent through the objection to the book from audiences and agents in the publishing field. Genette notes that paratextual function is to 'present and comment' on the text (45), and that epitextual formats such as correspondence, diaries, and authorial 'conversation' do not always fulfil such a function – instead, these aspects must be examined for 'paratextual scraps' (366). However, I argue that the link between author behaviour beyond the text and the text itself is heightened in the twenty-first century due to the changing author–reader relationships and the expectations of authors in terms of their presence on online platforms. The significance of social media's role in twenty-first-century authorship from 2010 onwards highlights the 'blurring' of private and public identities for authors (Laing 2017). Authors can deliver genuine insights into their lives on these spaces in an effort to establish their profile as an author, build their brand, sell books, and cultivate a relationship with both current and would-be readers. I therefore contend that an author's behaviour beyond the text acts as a paratextual threshold to their work, even if such behaviour does not explicitly 'present and comment' on their texts.

1.4 Research Approach

To achieve my research aims and answer the research questions, I conducted semi-structured interviews with authors, editors, and literary agents. This Element also brings together the disciplines of law and publishing studies to present a socio-legal analysis of the morality clause in practice. I establish how the clause operates in English and Welsh law before examining the implications of the morality clause's implementation in author contracts and the publishing field as a whole, drawing on two morality clauses provided by micro-publishers in England.

Purposive sampling was used to source interviewees who fell into the following categories: author, editor, literary agent. The descriptors presented in Table 1 indicate the perspective these interviewees give; any additional information will be provided throughout the analysis when relevant.

Publisher size has been determined via the European Commission's definition of micro, small, and medium-sized businesses (with anything above the stated employees and turnover considered 'large').[5] Within these categories, participants were at various stages of their careers/occupied different levels of the field, and this will be indicated when relevant throughout the analysis. Gaps in numerical order of participants represent allotted slots that were initially filled but ultimately did not take place during the course of data collection. Such reasons for withdrawal included Covid-19–related incidents, or concern from participants about their ability to discuss this topic.

Interview participants' responses to being included anonymously are significant to note here. Out of the twenty-seven participants interviewed, eighteen requested to remain anonymous, and one email interview participant did not indicate a preference when asked (therefore anonymity was granted as default). Some interviewees wanted to remain anonymous if they would not be able to see their used quotes in advance, and another interviewee did not express a desire to be anonymous or named. Out of those who wished to remain anonymous, there was an overarching theme of wariness of potential consequences should their names be attributed to their quotes, and an indication that anonymity was the condition for their honesty. I made the decision to present all data anonymously due to the majority of interviewees coming to this decision, as this makes the handling and presenting of data more consistent.

1.5 Structure of the Element

Chapter 2 argues that social media and twenty-first-century social contexts have changed the author–reader relationship, resulting in an increased focus on author behaviour beyond the text as a result. The chapter then discusses how this impacts an author's habitus in the publishing field, and demonstrates how author behaviour can manifest as a paratextual element to an author's work. Chapter 3 presents an analysis of the morality clause in

---

[5] See: https://single-market-economy.ec.europa.eu/smes/sme-definition_en.

Table 1 Research participants

Authors	Editors	Literary Agents
A01 (author with large publisher)	E01 (editor and owner of micro-publisher)	LA01 (also an author)
A02 (with large publisher)	E02 (at large publisher)	LA03
A03 (with large publisher)	E03 (at large publisher – education)	LA04 (previously an editor at undisclosed publishers)
A04 (with large publisher and editor with large publisher)	E04 (previously an editor with large publisher, now editor on a freelance basis)	LA05
A05 (with academic publisher and small publisher)	E05 (previously an editor with small/medium publishers, now freelance editor)	LA06 (previously an editor at large publisher)
A06 (author with small publisher)	E07 (previously an editor with large publisher, author)	LA07 (previously an editor at large publisher)
A07 (with large publisher)	E08 (at large publisher)	LA08
A08 (with small publisher)	E09 (at large publisher)	LA09 (previously a bookseller)
A09 (with large publisher)	E10 (at small publisher)	
A10 (author with large publisher)		

practice. It provides an examination of how the publishing agreement functions in the context of English and Welsh law to contextualise how the morality clause disrupts the publishing field. The chapter then explores concerns surrounding morality clauses and the inherent power imbalance between publisher and author, particularly when morality clauses contain ambiguous language.

2 Behaviour Beyond the Text and the Author–Reader Relationship

The relationship between authors and readers is, at its essence, a symbiotic one – one that, as Ng (2009) observes, 'transcends the boundaries of society, time and culture' (413). Yet such a relationship is not without its turbulence, and the complexities of the author–reader relationship can perhaps be best highlighted by examining its 'ups and downs', as it were. Using Arthur Conan Doyle as a nineteenth-century example demonstrates the extremities of both. The popularity of Conan Doyle's Sherlock Holmes character, initially appearing in the 1887 short story *A Study in Scarlet*, secured his status as a beloved, best-selling author with a devoted readership (Lantagne 2014, 267). Subscriptions to *The Strand* magazine increased in the wake of publishing the Holmes stories; readers wrote letters in abundance to Conan Doyle (and to 'Sherlock Holmes' himself), and some libraries increased their opening hours to cope with the demand of readers on publication days (Brombley 2017, n.p.). Yet, Conan Doyle showed signs of discontent with his writing, making it known his 'only fancy' was to write historical novels (Blathwayt 1892, 50). Upon expressing his desire to conclude writing his detective series, his mother, Mary Doyle, shrewdly observed: 'You may do what you deem fit, but the crowds will not take this light-heartedly' (Lantagne 2014, 268). Mary Doyle's prediction of how the 'crowds' would react merely touched upon the turmoil that followed. In the wake of Conan Doyle killing off Sherlock Holmes in the 1893 short story *The Final Problem*, readers expressed anger and disappointment. *The Strand* lost 20,000 subscribers, many readers wrote to Conan Doyle expressing their upset (Brombley 2017), and readers wore black armbands in the streets to mourn the fictional detective (Nussbaum 2014). The 'death' of Holmes and the subsequent reader reaction also attracted media attention, with one critic writing in *The Leeds Times* (1893, 4) 'I cannot get rid of the conviction that Conan Doyle has done a grievous wrong'. Conan Doyle's experiences with readers, both positive and negative, reflect how the interactions between authors and readers can change quickly, and how this relationship can influence an author. Skains (2010) observed that the relationship between author and reader is tied symbolically to the text: 'author and reader do not normally interact – except by means of the book or other published object' (96). In the case of the displeased 'crowds' and the 'grievous wrong' committed by Conan Doyle, it was the symbolic character of Sherlock Holmes that dictated the nature of the relationship between author and reader.

While Conan Doyle's 'ups and downs' with his readers took place in the late nineteenth and early twentieth centuries, when looking at author–reader relationships from 2010–2021 it would appear, at first glance, that little has changed. Readers continue to boycott authors when unhappy (Crawford 2022), they contact authors directly to let them know of their displeasure, and they demonstrate their disapproval in public-facing ways (Johnson 2021, 126–127). Yet, simultaneously, the author–reader relationship is much changed. This is in part due to the emergence of social media in the publishing field as a platform for both authorship and readership, and because the twenty-first-century author–reader relationship does not only revolve around, to use Skains' (2010) term, the 'published object' (96). When discussing the ways US publishers can exploit profit from 'around' the book by providing a speakers bureau service comprised of their contracted authors, Nash (2013) notes that while the book 'undergirds' the 'value' of an author's subsequent talk to an audience, it is not, in this case, the 'vehicle through which the actual revenue is conveyed' (n.p). I argue that while the book, to borrow Nash's term, 'undergirds' the author–reader relationship, it is not the sole vehicle upon which the relationship between author and reader is reliant today. The author–reader relationship is now influenced by an author's behaviour beyond the text. Readers can gain insights into such behaviours and practices in the first place due to the direct link readers have to authors via social media. Such a link ensures that authors are accessible to the public in ways never experienced previously (S. Murray 2018, 49).

Conversations surrounding the concept of 'separating the art from the artist' when authors are accused of behaving problematically mean that an author's opinions and behaviour can greatly impact their relationship with readers. Using J. K. Rowling and her readers as an example from 2020 onwards, it is not merely her texts that have affected her relationship with some readers but the behaviour she exhibits beyond them. The 'published object' (Skains 2010, 96) linking the author and reader is of course still a part of the author–reader relationship; as long as authors produce texts, this will always be the case. But no longer is it mainly issues directly related to the content of the text – such as plot, literary devices, or the killing of a beloved character – that drives readers to express their happiness or anger at the author. An author's actions, behaviours, and statements of opinion beyond the text now substantially impact the author–reader relationship. These aspects can also influence an author's relationship with readers who have not even read their texts in the first place. Alongside social media becoming increasingly important to the roles of authorship and readership, twenty-first-century social contexts have found their momentum on online spaces and lead to audience expectations as to how individuals with platforms – such as authors – behave.

This chapter investigates the changing author–reader relationship and readers' direct link to publishers and authors via social media, as well as the manifestation of the increased focus on an author's behaviour beyond the text. It explores how instances of problematic behaviour can impact an author's position in the publishing field, and argues that the strong link between an author's behaviour beyond the text and their texts themselves indicate how their such behaviour manifests as a paratextual threshold. Ultimately, this indicates a changing habitus experienced by agents in the publishing field – particularly authors. Gulledge (2011) describes habitus as something that 'explains the ability of an agent to understand and negotiate the field . . . It is this which informs "reasonable" or "unreasonable" conduct' (43–44). Reasonable or unreasonable conduct in the publishing field now encompasses author behaviour beyond the text and how publishers, alongside editors and literary agents, respond to this behaviour.

2.1 The Author, the Reader, and Social Media in the twenty-first Century

Ahead of social media's emergence in the field at the turn of the twenty-first century, Gardiner (2000) observed that author 'production' had transformed into 'author promotion' and argued the author brand had become as important to the selling of a work as the work itself (67):

> 'Customer loyalty' has to be cultivated through the author, the author is the brand, it is the author who has to be recognisable and built in as product recognition. If the representation of the

> author has been re-configured, so has his or her work. He or
> she has become a unitary sign for all the processes of publishing,
> and they in turn represent him or her. (68–69)

The 'author as brand' concept has increased in the years since Gardiner's observation. Squires (2007), giving an example of how the author as a 'brand name' manifests in the late twentieth/early twenty-first century, notes that an author's name is incorporated into an 'array of paratextual strategies' (87), and contends that 'brand images, particularly author brand images, work towards creating associations in readers' minds which may or may not be related to formal similarities in text' (89). As Royle et al. (1999) establish, the 'recognition' of an author is more common than the 'recognition of a publisher's imprint as a brand' (5). Yet, Gardiner (2000) also notes that the author brand can represent the publishers' brand in the eyes of consumers (69). The intertwining of author/publisher brands as observed by Gardiner, with the publisher ensuring 'loyalty' through the author brand, means publishers' reputations can be affected by the author brands they themselves establish and foster. From the 2010s onwards, the author brand encompasses an author's social media presence and the behaviour they exhibit beyond the text.

Authors are active producers of their own brand (beyond their writing) in the twenty-first century thanks to digital technologies. Simone Murray (2018) recounts the platforms utilised by authors in the twenty-first century: 'These digital accoutrements typically include a blog, a Facebook page, and a Twitter account, but can also span more arcane (at least for traditionally late-adopting literary authors) digital technologies such as podcasting [and] videoblogging (vlogging)' (35). Such is the nature of advancing technologies that, since the publication of Murray's foundational work, new digital platforms have emerged as ways for authors to establish their brand online, such as TikTok and Substack, while Twitter has experienced a rebranding and is now called 'X'.[6] In the years following the publication of this Element, no doubt my additions to Murray's observations will become outdated as new platforms emerge and existing platforms evolve.

---

[6] As it was still named 'Twitter' while conducting interviews for this Element, this is the name that will be used to describe the platform throughout this work.

The introduction of social media played a significant role in what was expected of authors from publishers regarding creating a suitable marketing platform and fostering relationships with readers. Clifton (2010) observed:

> Publishers now expect authors to have their own platform already in place, and they do not expect to build it for them. The platform itself has been redefined as an online/social media presence or network, and the author must have a built-in audience already listening to them. Some publishers will only sign an author based on the existence of a strong author platform ... The platform is a MUST HAVE, and authors cannot ignore the process of building one. (107).

Clifton's observation is not necessarily a definitive description of authors' social media expectations of the time: indeed, the involvement of a publisher in an author's online presence can differ, as Skains (2010, 100) notes during the same time period. Nevertheless, the perception that the online author platform was a 'MUST HAVE' (emphasis Clifton's) in 2010 suggests that the development of social media as integral to the role of an author has been evolving and changing for some time. As Thomas (2020) observes almost ten years later, 'maintaining a social media presence has become an expectation rather than an exception for contemporary authors' (99). Laing (2017) argues that authors primarily use social media for marketing, publicity and networking. To Laing, this blurs the lines between an author's 'private' and 'public' identities (256). An observation that emphasises this blur comes from Thomas (2020), who notes that the 'experience' of following authors over 'months or years' can 'provide readers with valuable insights into the everyday lives of authors and how authorial careers evolve, stutter, or change track over time' (104).

However, such a vast amount of insight into an author's life and exposure to their online behaviour can present an opportunity for negative interactions. Problematic behaviour from authors, particularly on social media, can have a negative impact on their publisher or present inaccuracies regarding a publisher's values. Laing's observation of the merging 'private' and 'professional' identities suggests authors could face professional consequences for personal social media content not related to their work in any way. This can be seen in the example of *Tynes* v. *Rare Bird*.[7] Tynes faced potential contract termination from their US publisher on the grounds of 'moral turpitude' for producing allegedly racist content on Twitter (BBC News 2019). The expectation observed by Thomas (2020) that authors should be present on social media was felt by all ten of the authors interviewed for this Element, with each of them using social media in their role as an author. Author A04 observed: 'I would love to be able to interact – like when we get proofs and stuff I'll definitely interact with people on Twitter.' A04 possesses a unique viewpoint in that they also worked as an editor in a large publishing house, and their understanding of the importance of using social media as an author, as well as a member of staff in the publishing industry, was clear. Interviewee A03 highlighted the pressure for authors to be on social media felt by those seeking to enter the industry: 'I wasn't on social media before I published a book so it was a very big change in my life . . . But I would say it's a really important part of the process for me now.' This insight demonstrates the pressure – exerted by both readers and publishers alike – for authors to have a social media presence, making them more accessible to current and would-be readers and is reminiscent of Laing's (2017) findings that 'authors feel a sense of compulsion to engage with social media – there is a commercial expectation and a financial pressure applied by publishers' (260). Murray (2019) also notes that social media allows readers a 'daily' or 'even real-time' communication with authors, meaning 'authorship thus stands at a fascinating point: at once sacralized more than ever and yet, in theory at least, never more accessible to a mass public' (38).

The development of readers and the way they interact with authors and texts in the twenty-first century has also been impacted by social media. Lawson (2020) provides a productive overview of the vast scholarship concerning twenty-first-century readership, and her evaluation of Overdorf and Barragree's 'five tiers' of readers in the early twenty-first century is especially insightful (58, 67; see also Overdorf and Barragree 2001).

[7] *Tynes* v. *Rare Bird Lit Inc*, Superior Court of the State of California, 6 June 2019 https://s3.documentcloud.org/documents/6143871/Natasha-Tynes-Complaint.pdf.

Lawson's evaluation of Overdorf and Barragee's final two tiers is relevant to the twenty-first-century reader my work considers. These two categories, summarised by Lawson, are as follows:

1. People who just enjoy reading – these are people who enjoy the look and feel of a book; who enjoy the tactile nature of the product; who admire the cover, enjoy the back cover, and see the product as part of the experience of reading.
2. Book lovers – this group value books intrinsically as objects in their own right, whether or not the books are actually read. This group cherishes the printed product and cannot conceive of a digital alternative, as the aesthetics of the product are just as important as the content. Books are owned and kept as loved objects. (67)

While these definitions also consider the relationship readers have to the materiality of books, these definitions reflect a wide range of readers relevant to this Element – namely, those who read for pleasure and have emotional investment in texts and authors. The observation that book lovers can engage with texts whether the 'books are actually read' is significant to note. In an age where readers can treasure a book they have not yet read,[8] readers can also engage with an author of a title they have not yet read, or ever intend to read, which highlights how the author–reader relationship has changed in the twenty-first century. Lawson (2020) observes that analysis of readership in the early twenty-first-century is, of course, unable to account for the development of social media and contends that this affects both the dissemination of information and the 'behaviours of readers' (68). Lawson also highlights the significance of online book clubs and readers creating communities on social media platforms to share reading experiences, illustrating the prominence of social reading in the

---

[8] The relationship between readers and books they have not yet read, whether or not they intend to read them, can also be seen throughout history. For example, Price's (2012) work on this phenomenon in Victorian Britain explores how the book could be displayed to demonstrate material value, amongst other social contexts (xiii).

twenty-first-century publishing industry. The development of social reading throughout history has also shaped how twenty-first century readers interact with each other and with authors. Regarding late-twentieth-century reading communities, Griswold et al. (2005) observe: 'Books are social products, but reading must also be taught; gatekeepers . . . steer reading choices; and for many people the reading experience is intrinsically social' (134). This 'intrinsically social' reading experience is heightened by social media and other social-reading sites in the twenty-first century. As Driscoll (2021) notes, 'social media allows for a new directness and immediacy in the relationships between readers, authors and publishers; one that is not dependent on mediators'. Social media, then, while providing authors with a platform, also provides readers with a platform. Editor E08 discussed this notion in their interview:

> I think readers are being able to be more vocal about what's problematic for them by Tweeting. I mean, mainly by Tweeting to be honest but also they feel they're more able to share that opinion with the publisher because they have more access to them . . . publishers and authors are being made more aware of the effect of their books on readers, and being able to get a lot more direct feedback.

Despite the expectation that authors will now incorporate social media into their roles, some interviewed authors expressed hesitancy at using social media to build an author platform and interact with readers. A06 in general felt frustrated at the lack of publisher support when it came to marketing titles. In 2017, Laing's findings reported a similar sentiment (265). Across the industry, there is a disparity in the support authors receive from publishers when it comes to marketing their titles, which depends on a multitude of factors, such as the publishers' resources and the money dedicated to an author's marketing campaign. The perception that publishers are not always equipped to assist authors on social media suggests that, should authors face new, changing expectations from readers as to how to conduct themselves online, then they may be left to deal with these changing expectations with little support. As well as this, the fact that authors are more accessible 'to a mass public' (Murray 2019, 38) suggests they are also vulnerable to negative interactions with this 'mass public.' A06 – whilst addressing the perceived power imbalance between publisher and author overall – noted that the publishing industry's approach to online marketing in general was 'ludicrous': 'It's like the shot-gun approach ... if you go to somewhere like Hay House publishers they'll only publish somebody that has – in the States, I think it's a social media platform, they're looking for 100,000 [followers], it's not about the content, the quality of the book.' While the UK Hay House submission page does not explicitly ask for 100,000 followers (though it does request 'authors with a strong platform through which to promote their work (for example, a significant email list)'),[9] A06's feelings reflect the pressure perceived by authors to be present on social media, and a belief that career opportunities could be made available proportionate to their success on the platforms. In their interview, literary agent LA04 observed: 'I think that social media has taken away a lot of authors' privacy and, I mean they've given it up willingly, but I don't think they understand how much they are giving up.' This observation raises the question of whether this privacy is given up entirely 'willingly' if authors feel the need to be on the platform for their career. Such a remark is indicative of the potential tension that can be created in the author–reader relationship due to the 'mass availability' of the author. While speculation and debate remains about the efficiency of an author's social media followers driving book sales, there still exists an expectation for authors that they should be available to readers on social media platforms. This often involves much unpaid and laborious work. For example, as Murray (2019) notes, 'Authors are also being lectured on the right *kind* of social media persona to cultivate. Merely bombarding one's Twitter followers or Facebook friends with publicity for a new title or upcoming in-store appearance is insufficient, even poor form; making proper use of the collaborative, peer-to-peer nature of social media involves genuinely interacting with one's followers' (50). Such a difficult balancing act not only exerts significant pressures on authors to perform 'genuinely' to audiences, but potential negative reactions to 'merely bombarding' audiences with details

---

[9] See https://web.archive.org/web/20220530082315/https://www.hayhouse.co.uk/guides/.

of their titles demonstrates that it is now not only the text that fosters a relationship between authors and readers. Kiernan (2021) observes that 'Marketing tactics on social media are often necessarily opportunistic in that they thrive on real-time conversations in order to promote engagement . . . the success of these publications seems to depend on the authors' networks and commitment to being vocal about their books' (38). Here, Kiernan notes the importance of 'real-time' conversations with readers alongside being 'vocal' about their books. This online 'commitment' – 'often unpaid' (Murray 2019, 50) – which requires a balance between 'genuine' engagement with readers alongside the promotion of their work can, for some authors, contribute to their book's success, especially if their publishers are not dedicating large marketing budgets to these authors.

Returning to Murray's notion that authors on social media are encouraged to engage 'genuinely' with readers, author A03 discussed their social media presence:

> I'm very active on Instagram and Twitter and I just joined TikTok . . . for my own enjoyment as an author, the connection with readers being a part of that, like a conversation, a community, a connection and . . . writing can be so isolating and social media can be so connecting . . . it's really lovely to connect to people who find the things that you write interesting, compelling, challenging, and I think that's why most writers want to write – to connect.

The emphasis on 'connecting' with readers being important to the process of authorship in general highlights that positive relationships with readers can be nurtured when an author has a knack for behaving 'genuinely' online. This 'connection' through social media is a result of the direct access readers have to authors on the platform, as Squires and Ray Murray establish in their work reconfiguring Darnton's Communications Circuit (2013, 4). Of course, such online engagement with readers is not an essential part of the process for all authors, and indeed not all authors succumb to the pressure of being present on social media. In these cases, readers cannot gain such 'valuable insights' as Thomas (2020) observes, into authors' lives 'over weeks, months, years' (4, 104). For instance, literary fiction author Sally Rooney has no social media presence as of 2021, and authors such as Becky Albertalli no longer run their own social media accounts.[10] Some authors have social media and use it solely for obvious promotional purposes,[11] in which case the authentic 'connection' noted by A03 and the 'genuine' direct link to the author is somewhat severed. Nevertheless, as this chapter has shown, having a social media presence is a pressure felt by many authors, which is why the aforementioned authors can be considered an exception.

2.2 Behaviour Beyond the Text

Such a vast amount of insight into an author's life and exposure to their online behaviour can also present an opportunity for negative interactions. Going back to Laing's (2017) observation of the blurring of 'private' and 'public' identities (256), some interviewees touched upon this concept. During interviews, authors were asked if their social media platforms were used in either a personal or a professional capacity, or both. A01 answered:

> I personally find it hard to separate the two because it's hard to know where your brand begins and you end. So for me it's a mixture of book stuff but also personal stuff because I think nowadays you can't really separate the two in my opinion . . . I think if you have an account just promoting your work it can feel a little bit spammy and like you're a bit robotic.

The use of 'robotic' reinforces Murray's observations that authors are expected to be 'genuine' in their online presence. As a result, in an effort to reduce being labelled as such, for A01 it is 'hard to know where your brand begins and you end.' A10 had similar feelings, but distinguished their online activity through identifying what they called 'publicity' mode: 'I think you can tell when I'm sort of getting into like publicity mode because I stopped Tweeting about Michael Sheen quite so much and start Tweeting about my book a little bit

---

[10] See the pinned Tweet: https://bit.ly/3yDOxjM.

[11] Authors sometimes establish this by making it clear via their username or author bio. For instance, changing their Twitter handle to '[Author name] Updates Only.'

more.' Yet, the 'genuine' nature of A10's personal use of social media – posting about celebrities they admire – contributes to their author brand, whether or not they are in 'publicity' mode. Editor E10 echoes this sentiment: 'An author is closer to their readers than ever before and that's the key point – the thing is that because of social media and Twitter, people are engaging closer together with people that they haven't met. An author personality is all part of the promotion of their work.'

These accounts from interviewees reflect Goldsmith's (2016) position: 'Factors such as an author's persona, online behaviour, political or social views, and role in prominent genre controversies can have significant impacts on readers' reception of their work, both explicitly and implicitly' (32). But, for other authors, the pressure to mix the 'genuine' with the 'professional' remains a prominent conflict. Authors must juggle this while maintaining the 'one-to-many' relationship with readers on these platforms, as Simone Murray (2018) observes: 'Now the author is engaged in one-to-many or even one-to-one real-time relationships with readers, providing updates on the progress of writing projects, plugging future in-store or media appearances, intervening in current political or cultural debates' (12). The inclusion of an author's involvement in 'current political or cultural debates' highlights the impact social contexts have on expectations placed on authors, and, as Goldsmith (2016) stresses, in 'the current publishing environment' an author's work can be impacted by sharing their political and/or social views (32). In 2016, Goldsmith surveyed speculative fiction readers to establish what influenced them to buy an author's titles. Goldsmith found that 57 per cent of respondents were likely to not buy a book due to an author's behaviour, and 55 per cent would not buy or read an author's books due to an author's social or political views: 'Many readers saw their purchases as an indirect endorsement of the author as an individual or their views', notes Goldsmith (2016, 39, 41). Such views do not necessarily need to be explicitly stated; they can be apparent via an author's behaviour, for example, by sharing what causes they support on social media. For instance, behaviour on social media being perceived by readers as problematic was apparent in 2019, when Gareth Roberts was removed from an anthology by Ebury as readers found and cited Tweets by the author in 2015 that contained 'offensive language about the transgender community' (Chandler 2019b).

Additionally, authors who achieve high levels of success in their career, accumulating large amounts of capital, can amass a large number of followers on social media. This means that they reach a mass audience via their social media activity and not just via their texts. Literary agent LA05 observed:

> If I buy a product or book or whatever it might be from someone whose views I disagree with then find their conduct in the public sphere problematic to communities that I care about, then by buying that product I'm giving them money and I'm building that platform, and I'm enabling, in some cases, danger and harm to people I care about, and communities that I'm invested in.

This comment suggests that the 'economic' aspect of the relationship between author and reader has an added depth in the twenty-first century – namely that, for some, supporting authors means 'enabling' them to continue having an influential platform. It is now no longer the mere act of publishing that provides authors a platform, but the social media following they can accumulate due to the social capital gained as an author. Social media manager Eva Recinos, quoted in *Bitch Media*, notes:

> A book is this physical, solid object that you carry around with you. The words are printed and that's it . . . On Twitter it's a whole different game. It's strange to think about how you can tell people about your favorite book/author and they can say 'She's hilarious on Twitter' or ' I don't really like what she Tweeted about x, y, z.' It's up to readers to decide how [an author's] social-media [presence] changes how they view a book. (Lewis 2019)[12]

This sentiment – that social media activity is now something that can impact a reader's reception of the author and their work beyond the 'physical, solid object' of the book – was reflected by author A10:

---

[12] *Bitch Media* has since ceased production.

> [There are] kids who are picking these books up and then going
> and Googling their favourite author. And what's the first thing
> that jumps out ... It's all your social media feeds, and it's the
> last thing that you posted. And if your hero is saying ... they
> don't like people who look like you or sound like you or have
> your kind of background, it must be absolutely devastating.

A10 here suggests that it is no longer only the physical book that links the
author and reader. An author's social media activity and online presence,
their life beyond the text, is now a significant aspect of the author–reader
relationship for readers who choose to engage in an author's online presence. In this way, their life beyond the text becomes an epitextual threshold
for their work. J.K. Rowling makes for a relevant example when it comes to
an author's life beyond the text as accessed via social media affecting the
way readers 'view' a book. Rowling has also used her social media platform
to discuss views that have caused splits within her readership prior to 2020:
for example, she was vocally against Scottish Independence ahead of the
referendum in 2014 (Flood 2014), and in 2016 her anti-Brexit stance caused
further divide amongst her readers (Elgot 2016). The reaction to Rowling's
comments online from 2020 onwards demonstrates how an author's social
media presence can take precedence over an author's texts when it comes to
the author–reader relationship, with readers who oppose her views calling
for boycotts and some refusing to read her work (Romano 2020).

With social media giving a direct link to authors and their publishers,
readers can use these platforms in an attempt to influence literary production,
with publishers, editors, literary agents, booksellers, and other readers in the
publishing field hearing their concerns. Observing this behaviour in readers,
literary agent LA05 argued:

> I am a proponent of voting with your wallet. I think that if
> someone's done something that annoys you, or distresses you,
> you have the right not to engage with their work, and you have
> the right to tell your friends not to engage with their work. I can
> say to my friends 'Look, I know you're a big fan of this author,
> but by buying their work you're increasing their platform.'

This observation links back to Goldsmith's (2016) findings that some readers perceive the purchasing of an author's work would be 'an indirect endorsement' of their views (39). In this case, the reader exerts their right not to 'engage' with the work; the author and publisher lose the reader's business. In the hypothetical scenario presented by LA05, the phrase 'I know you're a big fan of this author, but . . .' indicates that being a fan of the author and their work is not enough to surpass the problematic, 'distressing' behaviour they may have exhibited. This is a key change to the author–reader relationship in the twenty-first century. Editor E03 commented on insights gained into Rowling's views via social media: '[Rowling] could have held those views about trans people privately and still be published. And we wouldn't have known that that's how she felt.' When it comes to an author's behaviour and views, it is the expectation to perform 'genuinely' on social media that exposes readers to behaviours and views beyond the text in the first place. In times of significant social change, this can make for a turbulent setting for the author–reader relationship, particularly when readers' expectations of authors and publishers are not met.

While Rowling's case is an extremity due to her unique position of power in the publishing field, it is this very extremity that provides an insight into how the author–reader relationship can operate on a smaller scale. This smaller scale can mean that some authors – perhaps midlist, debut, or published by an independent publisher – feel a disparity in how they are able to present themselves on social media in comparison to authors with powerful positions in the field. As one author, A01, noted in interview:

> I know, for example, that some authors get told off for being too political, but in terms of kind of standing up for rights that they believe in. And I know they can kind of be censored in that way . . . If you're a big author who makes lots of money you can pretty much say and do whatever you want and if [you're] an author who doesn't, you're not as well known, you kinda get told that you're allowed to say and not say things. And so as an example I did actually have . . . at my publisher we had a sort of meeting that was

> talking about social media and how to conduct ourselves.
> We were told actively to not be political and that if we wanted
> to speak up about those sorts of things we had to create
> a separate account to our author account, which I found really
> interesting because we're basically being told how we were
> supposed to present ourselves as children's authors.

This observation from A01 suggests an awareness from publishers that an author's online presence is increasingly important to textual promotion and brand building, but that they are also aware of the potential polarisation of readers when authors discuss social and political issues, as seen on a larger scale with Rowling. A01 continued, explaining they had been told by their publisher to not be 'combative' when audiences (at events) asked questions about their text and race. A01 stated this 'made me feel like the persona that I had to give off is fake.' This incident highlights the significant challenges faced by authors 'not as well known'. As demonstrated previously, there is pressure for authors to be 'genuine' (Murray 2019, 50) in their interactions with readers, and this can involve speaking about social and political values. However, this contrasts with what A01 was instructed to do by their publisher, suggesting an awareness from this publisher that readers are increasingly aware of authors' social and political values and can exert power over other readers to influence reading habits or cause backlash if they disagree with these values, reflecting negatively on both publisher and author due to the intertwining of their brands. A01's observation also suggests that are different 'rules of the game' for authors depending on their position in the field and on whatever power they have gained via the accumulation of economic capital. Overall, A01's account here is suggestive of various tensions present in the author–reader relationship in the twenty-first century. They feel they have to present a 'fake' persona at times in order to foster a relationship with readers, and in addition have been instructed by their publisher on how to cultivate this relationship via social media.

2.3 *Author Behaviour Beyond the Text, Habitus, and the Morality Clause*

Ultimately, the changed author–reader relationship leads to an increased focus on an author's behaviour. Insights gained via social media combined with twenty-first-century social contexts and the close link between the author and the publisher brand present the opportunity for behaviour beyond the text to impact textual reception and cause financial and reputational damage for both author and publisher. When interviewees were asked why they thought the morality clause, and the act of terminating a publishing agreement due to author behaviour beyond the text, was reported by one UK literary agency to have increased from 2017 onwards (Wood 2018), many attributed this rise to social media and/or progressive movements, with some suggesting that both work in tandem to this end. For instance, as discussed in Chapter 1, some authors in the industry faced allegations directly related to the #MeToo movement, and these allegations of problematic behaviour impacted their position in the field. Progressive movements also impacted an author's habitus regarding their behaviour online. Pressure for authors to use their social media platform 'responsibly' by highlighting their support for progressive movements was felt by interviewee A03, an author who did not have social media prior to being published:

> Through, you know, seeing #MeToo and BLM, I started to be much more public, really, with it, especially my connection to Trans Lives Matter and BLM. And, I was also wary of virtue signalling as an author, and saying 'Oh I'm doing this, I'm supporting this charity' but some people, who on social media I really respect, sort of said 'look we really need you to support the things that we believe in' and so I really took that to heart . . . I see authors who . . . have platforms and use that to really champion other people and I sort of see that as allyship.

A03's observations highlight a direct correspondence between widespread social movements such as #MeToo and BLM and this author's habitus concerning their behaviour social media. A03 felt a need to use their platform to be an 'ally' to these causes due to the capital and platform they have gained as an author. Of more significance to this Element are the ways in which these movements can highlight instances of problematic behaviour exhibited by authors, particularly on social media. In interview, author A02 believed the visibility of authors on social media alongside progressive social movements had combined to increase morality-clause usage in the publishing industry: 'I think we are in the middle of an increasingly polarised society ... I don't want to say social media is to blame, I'd say social media is more like where it's happening. And a lot of movements have started to rise – like MeToo, like BLM and that kind of thing.' Meanwhile, author A09 observed that the increased visibility into an author's life via social media is impacting the way that they – and other authors – as agents in the field behave:

> The thing is the world has changed. Twenty years ago you could be awful and release your book and no one would know about it because even if you're in the newspaper, unless you did something just really terrible it'd be gone. But that is not the world anymore, you have to accept the world you live in ... if I go out ... around my neighbourhood waving a swastika, everybody will know about it. Within hours, people take pictures, it'll be on social media. That'll be straight out there and it goes straight to the people who buy my books. And I know that people who buy my books would not accept that.

In this hypothetical scenario, while the author's proposed problematic conduct took place offline, it is online that this behaviour could circulate, ultimately finding its way to A09's readers who would, in A09's opinion, object to this behaviour. In A05's words, social media is 'where it's happening' – 'it' being the reaction to an author's behaviour. This visibility A09 refers to means that part of this author's habitus as an agent operating in the publishing field requires knowledge of how to conduct themselves appropriately on social media (or knowledge that their behaviour beyond the text might be distributed on this platform). They must conduct themselves in a way that is not 'terrible' as a result. To A09, this represents a changing habitus as they believed that 'twenty years ago', before this visibility, their problematic behaviour would not be visible and would therefore be less likely to be scrutinised by their readers. A10 provided a second-hand, anecdotal account of an author's behaviour online being a point of focus for a potential publisher via a morality clause:

> One of my friends who is a literary agent . . . she said to me that she'd had a new contract come through for one of her clients and that there was a morality clause in it and she was going to have it taken out. Which was sort of mind blowing. I thought, 'Well, how can they possibly tell you what to do online?' This was specifically online this clause was for. And I thought it was just a one off. But since then, I've heard more and more authors saying that these clauses have cropped up in new contracts.

A morality clause specifically targeting an author's online behaviour is indicative of the changing habitus experienced by authors in the field, as well as publishers as a whole who now strategically decide to implement these clauses as a publishing practice. Such a morality clause suggests the importance a publisher places on an author's online behaviour and the potential reception of this behaviour from readers. It reinforces the notion that social media has changed the author–reader relationship, and that new expectations regarding an author's conduct have manifested as a result.

Overall, all ten authors interviewed for this Element believed social media to be either the reason for the increased use of the morality clause, or as a place where their behaviour could cause them to face repercussions from publishers. As mentioned previously, author A01 also discussed a training session held by their publisher which is indicative of this change – 'it was like: "this is a good way to Tweet, this isn't a good way to Tweet"' – further highlighting how external forces are changing an author's required habitus to navigate the field successfully, and in turn accumulate capital in all its forms. However, with each social media platform comes different ways to communicate and 'behave' and, as expressed earlier by A06, not all authors receive social media support and therefore must navigate these channels of communication independently. For example, when imagining a hypothetical morality clause in their own contract, author A04 raised the question of what is considered unreasonable conduct on Twitter: 'If I go on Twitter and . . .

I retweeted something really terrible and I didn't say it, is that cause for my book contract to be dissolved?' 'Retweeting' is the act of sharing another user's post on Twitter, and to A04 it is not clear if such behaviour would trigger a morality clause should one be present in their contract. The attention paid to this kind of behaviour was apparent in 2018 when Twitter users noted J. K. Rowling 'liked' a Tweet accused of conveying a transphobic message (Percival 2018). Tweets that are 'liked' on Twitter by a user (in this case, Rowling) are visible to others, and although Rowling herself did not make the comment, her perceived close association with it on social media raised discussions about her behaviour and opinions. Rowling later 'unliked' the Tweet, and the incident was described by her spokesperson as a 'middle-aged moment' (Percival 2018). There is also the question of when the behaviour occurred. Speculating on the perceived need for the morality clause, author A07 mentioned the potential for their past conduct and behaviour re-emerging across social media: 'I'd imagine [the increased use of the morality clause] was a wide mix of things, from #MeToo to various authors saying unsavoury things, to the relatively new fashion for digging out offensive old tweets written before the author was famous.' Here, A07 refers to the act of old social media posts from an author's past (still visible to audiences in the present, should they take the time and effort to look) being brought to attention. The incident with Ebury and Roberts concerned Tweets posted in the years prior to Roberts' involvement with the anthology they were later terminated from in 2019 (Chandler 2019b). While it has not been noted whether a morality clause was used or not, Ebury nevertheless removed Roberts from the project and terminated the contractual agreement. An official statement read: 'Comments made by the author on social media using offensive language about the transgender community have caused upset . . . and conflict with our values as a publisher' (Chandler 2019b). This incident once again demonstrates how the field has experienced a changing habitus: not only do authors now have expectations placed on their behaviours in the present, they also have expectations placed on their behaviours in the past. Or, they must take steps to conceal their previous behaviour by, for instance, deleting old social media posts.

Ebury's response to Roberts' Tweets reflect the argument from Sánchez Abril and Greene (2017) that the contracting party (in this case, Ebury) risk being seen as 'condoning' behaviour should they not distance themselves from the offending individual (24). Ebury expressly link their 'values' as being represented (via the conflict they present) by the behaviour of the author, indicative of the intertwining of author and publisher brand as observed by Gardiner (2000). As mentioned previously, Simon & Schuster attempted to lessen this perception by stating they did not 'condone' the 'discrimination or hate speech' Yiannopoulos was being accused of at the time. Editor E07 observed the perceived intertwining of an author's views and the publisher who platformed them: 'If you reveal you're a neo Nazi on Twitter, then that's a problem for your publisher. Unless your publisher's a neo Nazi in which case you're fine.' Commenting on instances of contractual terminations due to author behaviour in *The Bookseller*, Fewery (2021) writes that 'We've seen the lens turned on publishing decisions ... Grand Central cancelled the publication of Woody Allen's memoir. And Little, Brown did the same with Julie Burchill's book, after she posted Islamophobic comments on Twitter.' The incident with Julie Burchill prompted a response from publisher Little, Brown that was similar to Ebury's response to Roberts' behaviour in 2019. Little, Brown's statement read:

> We believe passionately in freedom of speech at Little, Brown and we have always published authors with controversial or challenging perspectives – and we will continue to do so. While there is no legal definition of hate speech in the UK, we believe that Julie's comments on Islam are not defensible from a moral or intellectual standpoint, that they crossed a line with regard to race and religion, and that her book has now become inextricably linked with those views. (Bakare 2020)

The linking of the author's views to the text is perhaps made here because the text in question is partly a memoir (Bakare 2020), but it nevertheless demonstrates that the publisher recognising the author's views as being 'inextricably linked' with the text means they could be, in the eyes of readers, also 'inextricably' linked to the publisher. Another instance of publishers explicitly distancing themselves from an author accused of problematic behaviour occurred in 2020. HarperCollins UK and other publishers dropped historian and author David Starkey after he was accused of making racist comments in July of that year (Flood 2020a). HarperCollins stated they were no longer publishing Starkey's upcoming titles and were reviewing the author's backlist titles in light of his comments: 'The views expressed by David Starkey in his recent interview are abhorrent and we unreservedly condemn them . . . Our last book with the author was in 2010, and we will not be publishing further books with him. We are reviewing his existing backlist in light of his comments and views' (Flood 2020a). A Hodder and Stoughton representative told *The Bookseller:* 'We unequivocally condemn racism in any form. We published a book by David Starkey in 2015 as a one-off project . . . We will not be publishing any further books by him' (Chandler 2020). Once again, the publisher's need to 'condemn' the views is an attempt to not only distance themselves from Starkey, but also from any potential implication that, by previously giving Starkey a platform, they condone such views. However, such moves can be met with scepticism. Editor E09 argued that 'I personally haven't witnessed an author lose their publishing contract for any reason other than the publisher has decided it is no longer financially sensible to publish the book . . . at that point there was no longer any money to be made from [Starkey] I would say.' David Starkey was also accused of racism following comments in 2011 (Flood 2020a) and 2015 (Weaver 2015), but it was not until Starkey's comments in July 2020 that widespread action was taken by his publishers. The recent distancing from Starkey took place during and after prominent BLM protests across the globe, and at a time in the publishing field where initiatives for Black authors and publishing staff were widely taking place (Roberts 2021, Romero and Martínez Figueroa 2021). E09's observations are reminiscent of Saha and van Lente's (2022) examination of publishing practices to increase diversity: 'Our sense was that stressing commercial value was an attempt to make a more rational case for diversity – as if the moral case is not enough to inform actual business decisions' (228). When it is apparent that companies recognise progressive ideals as a 'trend' to be exploited, audiences can perceive these motivations negatively, such as accusations of them participating in 'woke-washing' (Vredenburg et al. 2020, 455), whereby companies are not seen as being consistent in supporting progressive values throughout their institutions and structures and therefore are viewed as exploiting progressive ideals for profit or mitigating the loss of economic capital (Vredenburg et al. 2020, 455). Such a view was illustrated in author Roxane Gay's response to Milo Yiannopoulos losing his book deal: 'When his comments about paedophilia/pederasty came to light, Simon & Schuster realized it would cost them more money to do business with Milo than he could earn for them. They did not finally "do the right thing"' (Crockett 2017). While, as previously mentioned, it cannot be conclusively said that Simon & Schuster removed Yiannopoulos due to his behaviour, Gay's statement highlights the underlying conflict between commerce and social responsibility – when it is perceived by audiences that it may cost more money to continue down the 'wrong' path due to consumer activism, taking the 'right' one can be seen as a meaningless gesture. However, if a publisher utilises a morality clause, for example, purely to protect its reputation and finances, it still ultimately ceases being a platform for an author that some audiences may find objectionable. While such profit-driven motives can be met with negative responses by some consumers who expect consistent socially responsible practices, such a termination still demonstrates at least a degree of publisher accountability for problematic behaviour by removing the author from the platform the publisher provides.

As illustrated in this section, 'unreasonable' (Gulledge 2011, 44) conduct exhibited by authors (and the subsequent response by publishers) beyond the text can now impact an author's position in the field. Author interviewees in particular remarked on the role of social media when it comes to scrutiny of their behaviour, reflecting on the changed relationship between author and reader in the twenty-first century and the intertwining of the author and the publisher brand. An author's behaviour being perceived to be 'inextricably linked' to their texts (and, subsequently, to their publisher) suggests author behaviour can serve as a paratextual threshold to their texts.

2.4 Author Behaviour as a Paratextual Threshold

As previously mentioned, in 2021 author Blake Bailey's Philip Roth biography was pulled by W. W. Norton after Bailey was accused of sexual assault (Antonio Vargas 2022). Writing for *The Guardian* on this situation, Anthony (2021) writes:

> Even if the accusations relating to Bailey were all true – and he
> has denied that they are – should that affect our appreciation of
> his work, and whether or not it ought to be withdrawn from
> sale? If, for example, the designer of a vacuum cleaner was
> discovered to have a history of sexual abuse, would that
> vacuum cleaner be taken off the shelves?

Books, while also commercial products, hold symbolic and cultural value
which means, to commentators like Anthony, analyses of author behaviours
are heightened when compared to producers of non-cultural objects.
Recinos' earlier comments reflecting on author behaviour on social media
suggests readers can 'decide' how an author's social media presence impacts
how they 'view a book' (Lewis 2019). As discussed in Chapter 1, Genette
(1997) describes epitext as something that exists 'freely' in the 'social space'
(344). An author's behaviour exists in that social space: through traditional
mediums such as interviews, and also via online platforms such as social
media. With the 'blurring' of author's 'private' and 'personal' identities
online (Laing 2017, 256), an author's behaviour beyond the text can be
perceived to be linked to a text. This was demonstrated in interview with
editor E02, who argued that there is a direct link between the author's
behaviour and opinions and their work:

> I see a lot of like 'oh what's [their behaviour and opinions]
> got to do with their book?' You can't run past this, like, if
> you've got these opinions and you're sharing them, it's
> going to find its way into the book and at that point it is
> solely on the publisher what makes it out.

To E02, there is also degree of responsibility here for the publisher to
uphold, as it is 'solely' on them what 'makes it out' and is given a platform.
Editor E09 was less certain about the link between an author's behaviour
and their work, but still perceived a potential link in specific circumstances:
'Do I believe that someone who, you know, drinks excessively on their
Instagram should be dropped by their publisher? No. Do I think it should
come into a conversation if they are writing a book on abstinence and living
a sober life? Maybe.'

While E09 does not describe problematic behaviour here as defined by this Element, their comments are nevertheless insightful about how behaviour as a paratextual threshold can manifest. In this instance, to them, behaviour only potentially manifests as a barrier to an author's work if it directly contradicts the content of their work. Behaviour beyond the text can, of course, also positively influence readers, the paratextual threshold presented by such behaviour encouraging readers to engage with an author's work. Regarding social responsibility and Western brand activism, Vredenburg et al. (2020) argue that 'Social good is entering the mainstream. Driven by an increasingly polarized society, controversial issues such as the climate crisis, Black Lives Matter and the #MeToo movement are serving as catalysts for mainstream brands to define problems of social interest and refocus on doing social good' (456). This 'refocus on doing social good' is also observed within the publishing industry, as Fewery (2021) observes: 'Signs across the industry show that purpose is becoming more and more significant. And despite the slightly tricky relationship with brand, the book world will likely soon see purpose affecting their profits as well as their people.'

Authors can also 'refocus on doing social good' (Vredenburg et al. 2020, 456) beyond the text, as demonstrated previously when author A03 noted that they felt the need to use their platform 'responsibly' and be an 'ally' towards social justice causes. Toliver (2021), when exploring how epitext can help students better understand texts in the classroom, highlights how author's discussions about progressive social issues can be considered epitext for their novels when the content of the text aligns with these discussions:

> In 2018, four Black female authors – Dhonielle Clayton, Tomi Adeyemi, Justina Ireland, and L. L. McKinney – published young adult speculative fiction novels with Black female protagonists … within these novels, each author has discussed social justice issues … each of these authors has used their websites, Twitter pages, radio and online interviews, and podcasts to ensure that readers, if they choose, can better understand the underlying social justice metaphors in their speculative worlds. (84)

Toliver highlights how the wide breadth of social justice issues discussed outside of an author's direct experience and within the content of these works can be further understood should readers engage with these authors beyond the text. Toliver's use of 'if they choose' is significant here, referring back to Genette's observation that not all readers will engage with para-textual elements; for instance, not all readers read the foreword to a text (and therefore do not engage with the peritext) and, if an author's social media account and their life beyond the text is considered epitext, not all readers will engage with it or seek such insights.

With the intertwined author and publishing brands and the respon-sibility placed on publishers when it comes to platforming individuals, if enough readers choose to 'walk away' due to an author's perceived problematic behaviour, the publisher can face financial and reputational damage. The potential 'negative ramifications' (Alter 2018) of not redu-cing association with a problematic figure can be particularly prominent during times of social change. This led to the emergence of the morality clause and instances of publishers distancing themselves from authors perceived to have behaved problematically as a way for publishers to mitigate the damage (financial and reputational) if readers 'walk away' from the texts and, subsequently, threaten to 'walk away' from (or 'boycott', in the case of Simon & Schuster and Milo Yiannopoulos) the publishers as a whole. When shown an example of a morality clause detailing that an author's conduct could lead to contractual termination (but that did not specify exactly what behaviour would trigger the clause), author A05 noted:

> Let's take political leanings as an example – 'your political leanings are deemed to be egregious or rebarbative or nasty [and] could suddenly jeopardise your career as an author'. Up until really recently those things were always allowed to be separate ... In society, quite recently, in terms of an author's life ... that's something that could affect the rela-tionship between publisher and author.

A05 here notes that an author's 'political leanings' were once 'allowed' to be separate from their work and publisher, but now they perceive that this can affect the relationship between publisher and author, and impact the author's position in the field. This suggests that an author's behaviour beyond the text – in this case, their 'political leanings' – are paratextual thresholds to an author's work. Once two separate entities, an author's behaviour and the work they produce now come together to place new expectations on authors and the publishers that platform them.

3 The Morality Clause in Practice

Chapter 2 established that agents in the publishing field have experienced a changing habitus due to the increased focus on author behaviour. As a result of this increased focus on behaviour, morality clauses have emerged in the publishing industry as a tool to allow publishers to terminate contractual agreements should authors behave in a way deemed unacceptable in the eyes of readers and/or, as examined in this Element, should they exhibit problematic behaviour. This chapter presents a socio-legal analysis to demonstrate how the morality clause has impacted agents in the field. It first examines the object in which the morality clause appears, and the object that brings together publisher and author: the publishing agreement (or, the 'author contract'). By demonstrating how publishing agreements fit into the wider context of English and Welsh contract law, I present the argument that the manifestation of the morality clause in this legal context has the potential to further the existing power imbalance between publishers and authors. Then, the chapter draws on analysis of relevant case law; semi-structured interviews with authors, editors, and literary agents; and key incidents to assess the effectiveness of the morality clause when it comes to preventing and tackling problematic behaviour in the publishing field.

3.1 Contracts and Publishing Agreements in the Twenty-first Century

This section charts how the fundamentals of contract law in England and Wales impact the formation of publishing agreements, and how the ideal ways a commercial contract should be formed can differ from the reality of how they are actually formed and performed. In English and Welsh law, to form a legally binding contractual agreement there must be agreement from both parties. This is achieved when one party makes an offer (in this case, the publisher) which the other party (the author) accepts. Secondly, there must be contractual intention. Both parties are aware that they are entering into a legally binding agreement, and must conduct themselves as such. There must also be 'consideration' between the parties. Consideration is something of value that is given in exchange for the promise that makes the contract. To simplify the relationship and the concept of consideration, the publisher generally provides money (in the form of royalties and an advance) in exchange for the rights to an author's manuscript. It is significant to note that consideration generally need not be adequate (as established in *Chappell & Co Ltd* v. *Nestle & Co Ltd* [1959])[13] but merely sufficient. For example, if a publisher offered an author £1 for three full-length manuscripts, this would be considered sufficient consideration in this contractual relationship. Furthermore, the Courts do not concern themselves with whether a contract is a 'good' bargain or otherwise (as seen in *Retirement Villages Developments Limited* v. *Punch Partnerships (PTL) Limited* [2022]).[14] In 2015, the Society of Authors Trade Union outlined their 'C.R.E.A.T.O.R.' proposal for 'fair and reasonable' author contracts (Society of Authors 2015a). Their proposal calls for an increase in author payment due to the fact that the median earning for authors who dedicate more than half of their working time to writing is significantly lower than the UK full-time minimum wage. Since their proposal was established, author earnings have decreased further, to approximately £7,000 a year (Bayley 2022). However, their call for 'fair' remuneration is not one that would necessarily be considered by the Courts: first because sufficient consideration has been included in the contractual agreement, and, second, because of freedom of contract – nobody can be forced to enter into a legally binding agreement against their will.[15] Freedom of contract is the doctrine which allows parties entering a contractual agreement control over the terms. In other words, as described by Lord Diplock in *Photo Production Ltd* v. *Securicor Transport Ltd* [1980],[16] 'Parties to a contract are free to determine for themselves what primary obligations they will accept'.

---

[13] 'A peppercorn does not cease to be good consideration if it is established that the promisee does not like pepper and will throw away the corn.' *Chappell & Co Ltd* v. *Nestlé Co Ltd* [1960] AC 97, at 114–115.

[14] 'It is no part of the Court's function to rewrite a bad bargain.' *Retirement Villages Developments Limited* v. *Punch Partnerships (PTL) Limited* [2022] EWHC 65 (Ch) [98].

[15] If someone is 'forced' to sign a contract, this is known as duress and is not a legally binding contract. This is procedural unfairness, and does not concern the contents of the contract but rather the way in which the agreement was entered into by a party.

[16] *Photo Production Ltd* v. *Securicor Transport Ltd* [1980] AC 827.

Due to freedom of contract, the Courts do not typically intervene in contractual disputes when it comes to the terms of an agreement unless the terms breach statute law.[17] However, in reality, do all contractual parties truly get to dictate the terms of an agreement? Atiyah (1996) observes that standard form contracts contributed to a decline in both parties dictating contractual terms throughout the twentieth century, particularly when it comes to individual consumers entering contractual agreements: "The terms were imposed by one party, and the other had no choice but to accept them or go without" (16). This changing balance of power between parties was acknowledged by the Courts via the introduction of statute law, with consumers being protected from potentially 'unfair' terms in standard form contracts via 'key enactments' such as the Consumer Credit Act 1974 (Mitchell 2022, 35). Outside the remits of statute law, rulings still typically favour the tenets of freedom of contract when it comes to contractual disputes, despite standardisation and contractual relationships with little room for negotiation being commonplace in trade and commerce (Perrott and Forsyth 2018). The formation of the publishing agreement closely fits the most basic description of freedom of contract; there is the Copyright, Designs and Patents Act 1988 that must be adhered to, but otherwise terms included in the contract are up to the parties' discretion as enjoyed through their freedom to contract. Common law rulings have widely established that the law does not 'function' to 're-write a bad bargain', as argued in *Retirement Villages Developers Ltd* v. *Punch Partnerships (PTL) Ltd* (2022).[18] Therefore, the Courts would not intervene to increase author earnings, for example – campaigns from the Society of Authors on this matter require publishers to act. The same can be said about other clauses that are disputed due to their perceived 'unfairness', such as the morality clause.

---

[17] 'An Act is a Bill that has been approved by both the House of Commons and the House of Lords and been given Royal Assent by the Monarch. Taken together, Acts of Parliament make up what is known as Statute Law in the UK.' See www .parliament.uk/about/how/laws/acts/.

[18] *Retirement Villages Developments Limited* v. *Punch Partnerships (PTL) Limited* [2022] EWHC 65 (Ch) [98].

The following description from *Clark's Publishing Agreements* depicts the intention behind the contractual relationship between author and publisher:[19]

> The agreement between author and publisher is the lynchpin of their relationship. Both parties together need to ensure that it accurately reflects in detail not only the nature of the book they are discussing but also how each may exploit rights in that book and the financial rewards that they are entitled to. This cannot be over-emphasised; care and time spent on the contract prior to signature ought to enable each to avoid subsequent unsettling disputes. The contract should empower both author and publisher with the confidence that each party will do its job to mutual advantage. (Owen 2017, 1)

Overall, an author contract serves to 'grant rights' to the publisher 'in return for a promise to publish and (usually) remuneration' for the author (Jones and Benson 2016, 7). 'It is a relationship of trust in an industry that uniquely combines culture and commerce', notes Day (2023) on what the publishing agreement represents (2). The description included in *Clark's Publishing Agreements* presents an ideal scenario – particularly the emphasis on the 'care and time' spent on negotiations, and the 'empowerment' experienced by both author and publisher. However, this does not represent the reality of all relationships between publisher and author when it comes to the publishing agreement. Speaking about their experience with publishing agreements, author A10 demonstrated a detached approach:

> Negotiations happen almost behind closed doors. If there's any sort of big questions your [literary] agent needs to ask you … they will ask you for your permission to do that … And we don't actually sit down in the room and negotiate that. We just get updates like 'okay, we've had an offer for X amount of pounds. How do you feel about that?' … And I like that because I think it would really stress me out if I had

---

[19] A regularly updated industry guide to publishing agreements.

> to see every single little nitpicky detail on a not finished
> contract. It's stressful enough when I get track changes on
> a fiction document.

A10 discussing the 'closed doors' behind which the details of their contract are negotiated indicates the potential 'quietness' for the author when it comes to the negotiation stage, contradictory to the *Clark's Publishing Agreements* description of both parties taking care and time together, with the end result 'empowering' each party to be confident the agreement is mutually advantageous. A10's description also demonstrates the reliance on the literary agent for many authors in the field, but while the agent and publisher negotiate (and the agent indeed receives a percentage of the authors royalties, established in the contract between author and agent), it is ultimately a contractual relationship between the publisher and the author. A10's detachment from their own contract due to the 'stress' of the 'nitpicky details' suggests that the contractual terms and the ways in which the contract has evolved from the initial proposal to the finished negotiated agreement are not a priority to them, trusting their literary agent to negotiate an outcome that is in the author's best interests. However, the 'standardisation' of publishing agreements and the author's position in the contractual relationship (even when represented by a literary agent) can lead to fewer opportunities for negotiation. Regarding contracts in general, Mitchell (2009) observes:

> Documents are likely to be drafted by lawyers, not the parties,
> may contain significant gaps (either by design or oversight),
> may be signed without being read or understood . . . while the
> documents may record fully negotiated and genuinely agreed
> terms, they may also contain standard or boilerplate provi-
> sions whose inclusion is difficult to attribute the intentions of
> the parties in any meaningful sense. (682)

Jones and Benson (2016) also acknowledge that the formation of the publishing agreement is not necessarily suited to each individual author:

> Most publishers with any experience will have some kind of
> standard author agreement; in the case of a large publishing

> company it is likely to be a detailed printed or word-processed
> document of twenty or more clauses. It will, however, reflect
> that publisher's own experience: every clause will be there for
> a good reason, but it will – of course – be drafted from the
> publisher's point of view. (104)

As Jones and Benson note, publishers may tailor these contracts based on past experience. Jones and Benson's observation that 'every clause will be there for a good reason' further highlights that the presence of the morality clause in the publishing industry is a practice introduced due to the increased focus on author behaviour. As Pinguelo and Cedrone 2009 observed:

> Due to the proliferation of new forms of media, which has
> greatly increased the speed with which information is dis-
> seminated to the public, talented individuals are now sig-
> nificantly more scrutinized than they have been in the
> past ... [D]ue in large part to the Internet and new media
> outlets, a rather insignificant indiscretion on the part of
> talent can be broadcast to millions of people within minutes,
> or even seconds, of its happening. (367)

As discussed in Chapters 1 and 2, the proliferation of social media in particular has played a part in the introduction of the morality clause in publishing, with authors' lives being 'more accessible' than ever (Murray 2019) meaning that their behaviour is closely linked to their position as an author in the eyes of readers. Considering the use of the morality clause from 2017 onwards, literary agent LA07, discussing boilerplate terms in publishing contracts, noted:

> I guess they're [publishers] hoping that they can protect
> themselves in some ways by these morality clauses ... they
> can put these in now and contracts are standardising more
> and more. We are finding less variety between our contracts,
> we kind of feel like everyone's working for the same
> publishers ... publishers are all kind of becoming much
> more savvy about what their competitors are doing so they
> might as well do it as well.

LA07's first observation indicates that their perception of the morality clause is that it functions to 'protect' publishers, in terms of both their finances and their reputation – that is, their economic and symbolic capital. LA07 also comments that publishing agreements increasingly look similar from publisher to publisher. That publishers are 'savvy' to what their competitors may be including in their contracts suggests a general awareness of the disruption in the publishing field as a whole, and a need to adapt by implementing the morality clause in publishing agreements. This was the case with the inception of the morality clause in 1921, with other studios following the lead set by Universal Studios (Pinguelo and Cedrone 2009, 367). Jones and Benson's observation that the wording of publishing agreements 'reflect that publisher's own experience' also demonstrates that the morality clause's emergence is a result of disruptive incidents in the field, setting new standards of habitus in motion. In the US, while there was no morality clause present in Milo Yiannopoulos' publishing agreement with Simon & Schuster in 2016, a morality clause was reported to be featured in their publishing agreements in 2018 (Somers 2018). Somers reports on the wording of this morality clause alongside its implications for *Publishers Lunch*. The wording of the clause notes that should the author be 'publicly accused of the violation of law . . . or is otherwise accused of libel, slander, or defamatory conduct, or any other conduct that subjects, or could be reasonably anticipated to subject Author or Publisher to ridicule, contempt, scorn, hatred, or censure by the general public or which is likely to materially diminish the sales of the Work', the publisher can terminate the contract and '[recover] unrecouped amounts' (Somers 2018). Somers also reports that the clause contains wording stating that the publisher can exercise the clause 'or not, in the Publisher's sole discretion' (Somers 2018). The similarities between this wording and the wording of the very first morality clause (which also included the terms 'contempt, scorn or ridicule') are striking, particularly as the clauses are used almost 100 years apart. There are parallels to be noted between the emergence of the morality clause in 1920s Hollywood and twenty-first-century publishing, such as the polarisation of society regarding morals and behaviour, and audiences gaining new insights into the lives of performers beyond the screen in the twentieth century, and authors beyond the text in the twenty-first century.[20] Speaking about the increasing use of the morality clause in twenty-first-century US publishing agreements, Somers (2018) asserts the potential significance of the Yiannopoulos case on the morality clause's emergence in US publishing contexts, as well as progressive movements such as #MeToo and 'accusations of misconduct against a number of prominent people'. This suggests that the disruption faced by the industry due to readerly focus on authors' behaviours beyond the text accelerated greatly from 2017 onwards, implementing changes to the 'standard' publishing agreements across the industry. The presence of a morality clause means the author's life beyond the text now materialises in the very contract that secures the text's publication in the first place.

In interviews for this Element, each author was asked if they had a morality clause in their contracts. Of the ten interviewed, all were represented by literary agents and only two were familiar enough with their contract to explicitly know whether it did or did not contain a morality clause. Other participants either had a quick read of their contract before the interview, or looked while the interview was conducted. Many alluded to the fact they relied on their literary agent to negotiate their contract on their behalf. When interviewees were asked if they would feel comfortable negotiating the terms of a morality clause should it appear in any future contract, author A02 responded 'I don't think so – for a start, that would be my agent's job to negotiate that kind of thing. She knows better than I do.' A01's answer illustrated how they believed they were viewed by their publisher: 'I personally don't think I'm in the position in my career where I could do that. I don't think I'm important enough to any publisher to be able to do that.' Not feeling important enough to negotiate the terms of your own contract contradicts the very nature of freedom of contract in commercial contexts, where both parties 'are generally free to agree to whatever terms they like' (Perrott and Forsyth 2018). In 2015, Nicola Solomon, speaking for the Society of Authors, observed the potential power imbalance between publisher and author in their working relationship:

---

[20] In 1920s Hollywood this was seen in the rise of fan-magazines, with a '[sense] that fans were far more interested in the personal than the professional' (Barbas 2016, 29).

Authors are not in a strong negotiating position. Publishers are often large multinationals while authors typically work alone. Especially at the start of their careers they may have little or no advice and are thrilled to be offered publishing contracts . . . Individual creators are therefore at an inherent disadvantage when negotiating the terms of their contracts. (Society of Authors 2015b)

Author A01 was not 'working alone' – they had a literary agent to engage with publishers and advocate on their behalf – but the fact that an author with such advocation still feels they are not in a strong negotiating position, that they are not 'important' enough to any publisher to request changes, suggests that other elements are at play when it comes to an author's ability to negotiate contracts – namely, their position in the publishing field, and the capital they have accumulated (or have the potential to accumulate, as is decided by the publishing house when the terms of the contract are offered). Author A09, discussing the relationship with their agent and knowledge of their publishing agreement, said 'When I signed with [literary agent], he asked me what I wanted and I said I would like to be the client that you would choose to embezzle, because you can get away with it. Because . . . I don't understand it, it has no interest to me.' Answers such as these show how little agency some authors have, or feel they have, over the terms of their own contracts. As Day (2023) notes: 'The publishing contract has the capacity to fulfil or repress cultural and creative endeavours; however, in practice, it's hardly even looked at' (3). Even a satirical response to the HarperCollins morality clause in 2010 from Ursula K. Le Guin (2011) references an author's tendency to be detached from their contractual agreement: 'Because I did not read my contract with your wonderful publishing house HarperCollins carefully, I did not realise my moral obligations.' These discussions echo the Society of Author's findings that only 41 per cent of career authors sought legal advice before signing a contract, and that figure includes authors getting such advice from literary agents (Chandler 2019a). On one hand, nobody is forcing the author to sign the contract and enter the agreement with a publisher, but, on the other, the industry is so competitive and oversubscribed[21] that the act of getting to the contract stage is a rarity in itself, meaning authors could be unlikely to reject 'bad bargains',[22] as it were. This sentiment was expressed by author A05 who, when asked if they would sign a contract with a morality clause included, stated:

> I don't tick any of the boxes as someone who would be morally rebarbative or have some back story that could come out. I would just be inclined to say, look at [the morality clause] and think 'oh that's not really on, but fuck it I'll just sign it.' But ... the way literary contracts often work and it being so one sided towards the publisher, I'm always a little bit loath to rock the boat.

Out of the ten author interviewees, seven said they would sign a publishing agreement with a morality clause. One author, A03, who was unsure, said the presence of the clause would prompt them to get more involved in contract negotiations. A03 initially said their experience with their author contracts amounted to having a 'whizz through it' after their agent had already negotiated their contract. If aware of a potential morality clause, A03 would prefer to 'thoroughly discuss' the 'boundaries' of the clause. Four authors said they would sign a contract with a morality clause but only due to the pressure they felt to comply with publisher contractual demands. For instance, A05 added that 'I mean maybe there's a time down the line when/if I'm a very successful author that I can haggle over these things ... but definitely in my experience, and everyone in the literary community I know who is, I suppose, early-mid career, there's – it's a 'take it or leave it' with publishers often.' This example presents a similar image to that of a consumer in the twenty-first century accepting the terms and conditions of a product or service – otherwise they must go without – while reinforcing the role of

---

[21] See, for example, an account from a UK literary agent speaking to *The Guardian*: 'I take on a tiny percentage of the authors who submit novels to me, maybe three or four a year out of 35 or so submissions a week' (Barnett 2020).

[22] *Retirement Villages Developments Limited* v. *Punch Partnerships (PTL) Limited* [2022] EWHC 65 (Ch) [98].

power when it comes to an author's feelings of agency over their contractual terms. Author A08 gave a similar answer when considering signing a hypothetical morality clause: '[It] would depend on how desperate I was. If I really needed to get something published, and this seemed to be my only option, then yes I probably would sign it, and if I had multiple options, and was not desperate then there is no way I would sign a contract with a morality clause in it.'

These comments suggest authors may feel compelled to accept whatever terms are offered; A08's use of 'desperation' reiterates that traditional publishing is particularly difficult to enter. With some authors either choosing to remove themselves completely from matters of their contract or feeling they must 'take it or leave it', thus leading to feelings of pressure to accept a morality clause despite an author's objections, this creates an instance where the morality clause could further existing power imbalances in the contractual relationship between author and publisher. For instance, Editor E02, speaking about the morality clause in publishing agreements, argued:

> I think it's a contract like any other. If you were doing a job and started making racist comments to a co-worker you deserve to be fired. I think if you were given a contract for a book and you are making inflammatory and offensive remarks in places like social media then it's perfectly reasonable for your contract to be terminated.

This editor's observations that the morality clause is prevalent in employment contracts is correct: for example, a termination of an employment contract due to problematic behaviour on Facebook occurred in 2009 (Sánchez Abril and Greene 2017, 26). But, as explored in this section, the author contract is not a 'contract like any other' – it is devoid of the statutory protections found in employment contracts, for instance. This leads to the fear that the morality clause could be 'abused', a sentiment echoed by some trade and media reporting of the clause (Deahl 2018, Wood 2018). Simultaneously, the very existence of the morality clause reveals a fear of the author from the publisher – publishers 'fear' the financial and reputational repercussions should they find themselves associated with such authors. Behaviour can thus manifest as an economic consideration.

Economic factors are a notion that, Day argues, when discussing their role as an editor, present 'hurdles that challenged the trust between me and my own authors, and I [find] it difficult to balance my authors' interests and concerns with the publisher's' (Day 2023, 101). Publishers also have a position of power when deciding whether or not to exercise the morality clause should it be potentially breached. On the use of the morality clause in English sports contracts, Blackshaw (2003) notes:

> One important practical consideration in deciding what to do is the effect the breach of the 'morality clause' may have on an ongoing marketing, promotional and advertising programme in which the particular endorsement by the particular sports personality is a key and integral part. In other words, there can be occasions where it may be better not to exercise the right of termination but carry on with the promotion. Perhaps a case of any publicity – including bad publicity – being better than none at all. This, of course, is a difficult call to make in practice! (137)

Blackshaw further states that the morality clause is a termination right not an obligation, reinforcing the notion that the contracting party who is deemed to be the arbiter of the behaviour has the power to make the 'difficult call' of whether or not it is considered worth it to trigger the clause and disassociate themselves from the, for instance, problematic party. Perrott and Forsyth (2018) observe that 'the debate around morality clauses reaches to the heart of the doctrine of "freedom of contract"', and conclude that '[contracts] can often result in one party suffering a significant detriment. The court understands that contention and calamity are a natural part of the cut and thrust of business' – a reminder that Courts do not intervene to ensure that the terms of the contract make for 'good' bargains. This is pertinent when it comes to concerns surrounding morality clauses that are perceived to contain ambiguous language.

3.2 The Ambiguous Morality Clause and Author Behaviour

Ambiguous morality clauses that do not specify what behaviour might trigger the clause, or state when the offending behaviour could take place, have been a concern since its inception. To illustrate, I have composed what a vague and ambiguous morality clause used in the publishing industry could look like:

> [Publisher] will terminate this Agreement with immediate
> effect if the Author acts or is accused to have acted in a way
> that could injure [publisher's] or the Work's reputation or
> may otherwise be detrimental to the success of the Work.

Ambiguous clauses such as these leave room for doubt concerning how the contracted author should behave and what kinds of behaviour may lead to the termination of their contract. It is argued by some that ambiguous, vague morality clauses may not be deemed enforceable should their use be contested by the offending party, as noted by Blackshaw (2003) when discussing the use of morality clauses in the British sports industry:

> Such [morality] clauses need to be expressed in precisely
> defined terms in order to avoid them being held to be legally
> unenforceable on the grounds of vagueness and uncertainty.
> A general clause in general terms requiring a sports person-
> ality not to behave 'badly' . . . may lack such precision and,
> ipso facto, enforceability. (135)

The ambiguity of one of US publishing's earliest morality clauses was highlighted in 2010, when HarperCollins introduced it into their publishing agreements. Some figures within the industry expressed concern regarding the notion that an author's behaviour should affect their publishing output, including Ursula K. Le Guin (2011) in her aforementioned, satirical open letter: 'I would feel so terrible if I damaged the reputation or sales of my Work, or your reputation. You are my Role Model. Please believe me, your loyal and obedient author'. Such comments illustrate the perceived power dynamic between publisher and author – the 'loyal' and 'obedient' author here immediately adhering to these new expectations demanded of them by their contract. The HarperCollins morality clause that Le Guin refers to was submitted to the newsletter Novelists Inc. in November 2010 for analysis. The clause reads:

> If [. . .] Author's conduct evidences a lack of due regard for
> public conventions and morals, or Author commits a crime
> or any other act that will tend to bring Author into serious
> contempt, and such behavior would materially damage the
> Work's reputation or sales, Publisher may terminate this
> Agreement and, in addition to Publisher's other legal reme-
> dies, Author will promptly repay the portion of the Advance
> previously paid to Author, or, if such breach occurred
> following publication of the Work, Author will promptly
> repay the portion of the Advance which has not yet been
> recouped by Publisher.[23]

While this clause does include, for instance, a specific reference to commit-
ting a crime ('prohibitions such as acting "illegally" tend to pass muster',
comments Blackshaw [2003] when discussing the morality clause in the
context of English and Welsh law [136]) issues of ambiguity still arise with
the use of 'public conventions and morals' given the wide breadth of
behaviours this could cover. Vague terms also include 'materially damage'
the 'Work's reputation or sales' as such impact can be difficult to measure
(Sánchez Abril and Greene 2017, 41–42). Stein presented analysis on this
clause for Novelists Inc. in 2010, concluding: 'The author should attempt to
refine and narrow the language of the morals clause so as to exclude
behaviours which, while obviously immoral (e.g. an extramarital affair),
are unlikely to damage sales of the author's book' (Novelists Inc. 2010).
Such conclusions raise questions about what behaviour could 'damage the
sales' of an author's book or what behaviours could, although 'obviously
immoral', be overlooked by both publisher and audiences.[24]

---

[23] Novelists Inc. 2010. Email newsletter to subscribers, November 2010, Vol. 21,
No. 11.

[24] There is a notable exception here with morality clauses implemented by religious
publishers – for example, Benny Hinn was 'sued' by his publishing company in
2010 for violating the terms of his morality clause due to having an extramarital
affair (Harris 2021). However, this incident took place within a religious publishing
context, which is outside the parameters of this Element.

Overall, literary agents interviewed for this research stressed they would advocate against such an ambiguous clause in a client's contract. Writing on the morality clause in 2009, Pinguelo and Cedrone suggest 'broad' clauses are in the contracting party's best interests, as 'the company seeks to give itself extensive flexibility to terminate the talent agreement for any potentially damaging conduct of the talent' (370). Such implementation of the clause has been acknowledged by UK literary organisations. The Society of Authors' stance on the morality clause in 2017 reads:

> These [morality clauses] seem to us far wider than is necessary to protect a publisher's legitimate interests. They are impossibly wide: an author could be in breach for being indirectly involved in something which the publisher thought may be damaging to its reputation. We particularly dislike the fact that the test is often not objective but allows the publisher in its sole opinion to decide that something is damaging. We suggest to authors that these clauses be deleted in their entirety and, failing that, that they ask for assurances and amendments that make it clear that the provision would be invoked only in extreme and cynical cases. (Society of Authors 2017)

The Society of Authors' advice that such ambiguous clauses be 'deleted in their entirety' suggests that a 'wide' morality clause puts authors at a disadvantage in their relationship with publishers. Editor E05 discussed such a precarious position due to the many behaviours that could trigger a morality clause, and the severity assigned to such behaviours from the perspective of a publisher:

> If you publish an author and you discover that they're a paedophile, do you want to keep publishing that author? Maybe not. If you discover that someone has been embezzling funds from a charity . . . Do you still want to publish them again? I think maybe not. If you discover that they cheated on their spouse and bragged about it, or they got drunk and said something stupid once . . . You know, you

might think 'no, that's idiotic' but it wouldn't damage the relationship [with publishers]' . . . the spectrum of sorts of things people do – different decision makers will draw the line in different places. And it has to be partly a commercial decision. How will we look as a publisher; we are seen to be amplifying the voice of a person who is widely known to have done X or Y.

E05's observation highlights the link between author and publisher when it comes to authors' lives beyond the text by referencing how publishers want to be seen when it comes to 'amplifying' a voice known to have exhibited certain behaviour. The acknowledgement of the 'spectrum' of behaviour and the fact that 'different decision makers will draw the line in different places' indicates how, should an ambiguously worded morality clause be used, it is not just the author behaviour in question that is not clear, but also the way this behaviour will be received by each individual publisher.

Many interviewees referenced 'scales', 'spectrums' and 'grey areas' when it came to behaviour that might trigger a morality clause. Literary agent LA09 observed: 'It's a sliding scale . . . isn't it? Like some views are more heinous than others, and yet . . . the question is, who decides?' Gallagher (2016) observes that 'Moral turpitude clauses when used in any industry can also be ambiguous, especially since community standards of morality are constantly changing. In practice, defining moral turpitude seems to have adopted the 'I know it when I see it' approach' (109). An 'I know it when I see it' approach is also present in other aspects of the publishing industry, as Squires (2020) illustrates when it comes to commissioning editors deciding which titles to acquire (254). Squires' investigation into the 'gatekeeping orientation' of editorial practices revealed that editors sometimes demonstrated an 'instinctive' approach when identifying titles suitable or not for commission (254). These instincts, Squires argues, are actually learned behaviour; the habitus 'of' the editor that, as Gulledge et al. (2015) would describe, 'incorporates the particular logic of the field' (639). Such editorial instincts can launch an author's traditional publishing career, while such instincts on the part of the publisher regarding behaviour by an author can, as suggested by Harris for *The Bookseller*, 'kill a career' (Wood 2018). The very presence of the morality clause, whether ambiguous in its wording or not, suggests a new form of retrospective gatekeeping: while an author's work may give them a foot in the door, their behaviour has the potential to see them back out of it. Their behaviour can also serve as a barrier for getting into the industry, as literary agent LA01 argued: 'I, personally as an agent, if I knew somebody had particularly misogynistic views or homophobic views then I wouldn't take them on.' Literary agents are, of course, entitled to work with authors who they believe will be a good fit for a productive, working relationship. As Mandy Little (2011) notes, reflecting on the author-agent relationship: 'It's often a very personal relationship; there is chemistry and you understand one another' (22). An author's potentially problematic behaviour impacting their entry to the industry can only occur if the behaviour precedes (or makes itself known during) the author's interaction with the agent or, further down the line, the editors. While such behaviour can be revealed within established social networks, social media also affords a chance for such behaviour to become visible.

3.3 Negotiating the Ambiguous Morality Clause

When faced with an ambiguous morality clause, the literary agents interviewed for this Element spoke about their negotiation techniques – namely, negotiating for clear, specific morality clauses, which partly ensures that they, not just the publisher, determine what constitutes 'moral behaviour' when negotiations are successful. Literary agent LA05 explained:

> The problem with the morality clause is that it's vague . . . anything that leaves you in a grey zone is dangerous in the long term should conflict arise. So basically what I did was add as much wording as possible to push the vagueness in the direction I wanted it to go . . . I wanted the allegations to be widespread, I wanted them to be credible. I wanted to make sure that they had been investigated by the contracted party and found to carry weight before the contracting party was able to act on them. I wanted them to demonstrate that the allegations could have a significant and material effect on the projected sales of the work.

Such efforts to prepare for any 'conflict' demonstrates the overarching fear of the morality clause's potential to be utilised against authors; it is 'dangerous' in its vagueness when it comes to LA05's client's position in the publishing field. LA05 discussed their thought process behind the negotiation:

> [I] negotiated a contract between a client of mine and a publisher that my agency hadn't done a contract with before, which meant the morality clause was fresh ground. And normally, a UK contract doesn't have a morality clause. Initially I tried to have it taken out . . . And when the publisher said they couldn't take it out – it's standard on all their contracts with everyone they contract with . . . I built it up.

LA05's experience of a publisher refusing to remove the clause in its entirety highlights that, for some publishers, the morality clause is now a consistent practice in the aftermath of changing social expectations from audiences and an increased focus on author behaviour. Fighting for more specificity in this area, the agent asks for 'credible' allegations, and argues that the publisher should be responsible when proving exactly how such allegations could have a 'significant' effect on 'projected' sales of the work. In the United States, the *Nader* v. *ABC TV Inc*[25] case notoriously involved a wide-reaching morality clause that the Courts nevertheless upheld. The clause stated that the contract could be terminated should the talent do anything 'which might tend to reflect unfavourably on ABC' (Pinguelo and Cedrone 2009, 370). The widescale press coverage of the plaintiff's behaviour was deemed to be sufficient (Sánchez Abril and Greene 2017, 37–8). LA05's negotiation illustrates that when it comes to ambiguous morality clauses, it is not only the vague language determining the author's behaviour that could be disadvantageous to the author, but also the wording that suggests what impact this behaviour might have on the publisher as a whole.

As mentioned previously, Blackshaw (2003) asserts that ambiguous morality clauses can lack 'enforceability' (135). While, as mentioned, freedom of contract ensures that 'bad bargains' are not of concern to the Courts, there must also be a meeting of the minds *(Consensus Ad Idem)* between

---

[25] *Nader* v. *ABC Television, Inc.*, 330 F. Supp. 2d 345 (S. D. N. Y. 2004).

parties. Meeting of the minds occurs when there is true assent between both parties concerning the intent and terms of the contract:

> One cannot doubt that, as an ordinary rule of law, an acceptance of an offer made ought to be notified to the person who makes the offer, in order that the two minds may come together. Unless this is done the two minds may be apart, and there is not that consensus which is necessary according to the English law [. . .] to make a contract. *Carlill* v. *Carbolic Smoke Ball Company* [1893].[26]

If the language in a morality clause is ambiguous, how can there be true contractual assent between parties? In this way, the minds of both parties do not 'come together' as they instead perceive the meaning of the clause differently. If such ambiguous morality clauses were deemed unenforceable, then it stands that publishers' attempts to alter their practices in the wake of changing social expectations are not necessarily effective in these instances. For example, as Sánchez Abril and Greene (2017, 38) observe, in the US case *Dias* v. *Archdiocese of Cincinnati*[27] it was ruled that the included morality clause was considered a breach of contract because the clause in question did not specifically describe the act which triggered the plaintiff's termination and the court concluded a 'meeting of the minds' had not taken place (Sánchez Abril and Greene 2017, 38). However, even when ambiguous clauses are implemented into contractual language, meaning there may be scope to contest it on the grounds that there has been no meeting of the minds, literary agent LA07 observes that many authors may not be in the position to do so:

> Often it comes down to who has the most money in this situation. And who has actual legal support, which if you've got a big, big, author, the publisher will probably back down. If you've got a big, big publisher the author probably won't be able to make themselves heard. They don't have any kind of

[26] *Carlill* v. *Carbolic Smoke Ball Co* [1893] 1 QB 256 [269] (Bowen LJ).

[27] *Dias* v. *Archdiocese of Cincinatti*, 1:11-cv-00251, (S. D. Ohio 2011).

financial backing to challenge it . . . I feel like publishers can use this against, say, the bottom 90 per cent of authors, but the top 10 per cent – by which I mean financially – would kind of be protected from them if they if they wanted to fight it.

LA07's comments echo the wider concern about authors' contractual negotiating position, also noted by The Society of Authors (2015a), who campaign for contract terms that do not inherently place authors as the weaker bargaining party. Such an instance demonstrates how the morality clause works to further an already existing power imbalance between publisher and author; in this instance, even if the morality clause is not utilised effectively via its ambiguous wording, LA07 asserts that many authors would not necessarily have the resources to 'challenge it'. Literary agents interviewed for this Element explained how they attempt to either negotiate ambiguous morality clauses out of contracts or negotiate for more specific language. LA03 commented on this imbalance, echoing LA07's concerns: 'The problem with [morality clauses] is simple – which is that publishing is a business of Davids and Goliaths . . . Just by sheer economic power, there just aren't very many authors who can afford to fall into legal dispute with a publisher.' Two morality clauses in use by micro-publishers in England were collected for this research, and both of them utilised a degree of specific language that mitigates the perceived power imbalance between publisher and author (on top of the already mitigated power imbalance due to their position as small, independent presses). Morality Clause A, provided by interview participant E01, states 'We can terminate this Agreement [. . .] If you are convicted of any criminal offence that would bring the Publishers into disrepute.' 'Convicted of any criminal offence' is the only stated behaviour that can trigger the clause, and the follow-up that such offence would 'bring the Publishers into disrepute' contextualises the criminality in question. The additional wording stating the offence must bring the publisher into 'disrepute' suggests – although admittedly does not explicitly state – crimes of a more serious nature: those that might warrant reporting in the media, for instance. The requirement of being convicted for a crime suggests that it must take place from the point of the contractual agreement onwards. Presumably, the publisher would not commission an author convicted of such a crime should that be disclosed prior to the contractual relationship (although it should be noted that there is not a requirement to disclose such information in this context, and the clause makes it unclear what happens if an author has been accused of a crime but has not yet been to trial). However, other issues still arise with such specific wording, primarily the use of the morality clause when it comes to criminal convictions. LA04, having encountered the morality clause when negotiating with US publishers, noted:

> You know there are lots of crimes that people get convicted of that have nothing to do with their publishing and there are lots of times that people . . . are convicted unfairly . . . Well, in America, if you are a Black person you are far likelier to be convicted of a crime. I mean, I'm sorry. It's not even about conviction. You are far likelier to have been considered to have committed a crime than a White person so that language right there – and I have brought this up with publishers in the past and they have adjusted the language sometimes because they don't want to be seen as being racist . . . I think it opens the publisher up for accusations of racism that they would prefer not to be levied at them.

This raises concerns about the morality clause's existence across industries when such power imbalances inherently exist within legal systems, and when abuse of power can be exercised over marginalised communities. Such a thread of investigation is outside the scope of this Element, as it concerns inequality and hierarchies present within legal systems instead of merely within the publishing field. Nevertheless, this concern indicates another way in which the morality clause, whether ambiguous or otherwise, can contribute to the power imbalance between publishers and authors – specifically, in this case, marginalised authors. This is significant to note in the current contexts in which the morality clause has emerged in the twenty-first century. Problematic behaviour encompasses behaviour that is harmful to marginalised groups, and yet the morality clause itself has the potential to reinforce structural inequality found in legal systems. In this way, the morality clause itself can be considered problematic.

Throughout the interviews with authors who did not have a morality clause in their author contracts, the concept of an ambiguously worded clause created a general sense of wariness. When shown an ambiguous morality clause, author A05 observed that 'It's putting the judgement in the corner of the publisher which . . . could be used in a very negative way. Without much evidence, without much substance . . . if I had that in my contract I would . . . on a point of principle almost, I'd question it I think'; while author A08 remarked 'I would personally be quite concerned if I had something like this built into my contract. It feels like kind of easy out potentially for a publisher.'

The 'easy out' comment here is reminiscent of a literary agent who spoke to *Publishers Weekly* about the morality clause in US publishing in 2018, speculating publishers could 'use this clause to get around what's legal and fair' (Deahl 2018). Another concern raised by authors was the shifting standards of morality within the publishing house itself. A03, building on why they would be unsure about signing a morality clause, noted the worry about their potential allyship of marginalised communities being something that could trigger the clause should publishers' definition of 'morality' change:

> I support BLM and so I would want to make sure for example that my support of the movement and of the charities and my public ability to support those would not contravene that morality clause. And I would want to know what happens for example if a new person comes into my publisher who might have very radical different views to mine. What is the due process for morality? . . . I would want some examples of what that could potentially look like.

However, it could be argued that, in English contract law, the slightly more flexible allowance for contract interpretation and the lack of court involvement when it comes to the terms of a contract means that even a morality clause with ambiguous language could be interpreted accurately and thus a meeting of the minds is achieved. Regarding contract interpretation, Lord Wilberforce, in *Reardon Smith Line* v. *Hansen-Tangen* [1976],[28] established the 'factual matrix':

[28] *Reardon Smith Line* v. *Hansen-Tangen* [1976] 1 W.L.R. 989 (HL) [995–997].

> No contracts are made in a vacuum: there is always a setting in which they have to be placed [...] In a commercial contract it is certainly right that the court should know the commercial purpose of the contract and this in turn presupposes knowledge of the genesis of the transaction, the background, the context, the market in which the parties are operating [...] What the court must do must be to place itself in thought in the same factual matrix in which the parties were.

Building on Wilberforce's 'factual matrix', Lord Hoffman established a philosophy of contractual interpretation should contractual disputes arise via five principles. These five principles of interpretation can be seen in *I. C. S.* v. *West Bromwich Building Society* [1998].[29] To summarise:

1. The court must consider what a reasonable person, with the same background knowledge that was reasonably made to the contractual parties at the time of the agreement, would take the wording in the contract to mean.
2. The 'background information' in question includes all relevant information that the parties had access to and would inform the way the language is used in the contract and would be interpreted by a reasonable person.
3. The 'background information' in question does not include any pre-contractual negotiations.
4. The intent of the contract may be different from the literal meaning of the words used, and the courts should not only take the literal meaning of words into consideration.
5. It should be considered that linguistic mistakes might have been made in the formation of the document, and in this case the courts do not need to consider 'an intention which they plainly could not have had'.

When considering Hoffman's first and second principles of interpretation, it could be argued that the meaning of a morality clause in a UK publishing contract from 2010 onwards can be determined within the context of

[29] *I. C. S.* v. *West Bromwich Building Society* [1998] 1WLR 896 (HL) [912–913].

the publishing industry: the twenty-first-century social contexts discussed throughout this Element that have generated a perceived need for the morality clause, and in particular the 'problematic' behaviour and views that lead to widescale objection.[30] A06, who believed a morality clause would be the 'least' of their problems, stated:

> I honestly think you have to look at it as common sense. They're not going to go finger wagging if somebody is doing something inappropriate on a beach, it's going to have to be the instant it is going to hit the headlines whether it's on Twitter like that YA writer I told you about, so anything racist – boom, you're out.

LA01, who was an author prior to become a literary agent, also expressed a similar sentiment: 'I have had [morality clauses] in my own contracts and I've accepted them, simply because I write kids' books and I'm really well behaved. So I feel very safe signing them.' These comments suggest these participants feel there are rules to follow; they see themselves as being aware of the required and shifting habitus and feel that they are sufficiently supplied with the relevant facts and contexts to determine how not to trigger a morality clause, even if the wording of a clause does not include specific behaviours and parameters. Such observations further reinforce the notion of changing 'unspoken rules', or habitus, operating within publishing, with author A06 confidently stating 'I understand the rules of the game. The publisher is a brand. The bigger the publisher the more they'll protect their brand.' Relevant cases of interest across jurisdictions could also be potentially drawn upon to interpret a perceived

---

[30] Objections to Hoffman's rules of interpretation include the notion that 'judges are not necessarily well-placed to determine what commercial common sense requires' (Sumption, as cited in Denis-Smith 2017, n.p.). This can be particularly apparent in industries that operate uniquely. For instance, in the US, as part of the Supreme Court case attempting to stop the Random House acquisition of Simon & Schuster (*PRH* v. *DOJ*), much of the inner workings of the industry had to be explained. See accounts of this as reported by Harris et al., for *The New York Times* (2022): www .nytimes.com/2022/08/19/books/prh-penguin-random-house-trial.html.

ambiguous morality clause. *Tynes* v. *Rare Bird Ltd*[31] saw Tynes' US publisher attempt to terminate their contractual agreement on the grounds of 'moral turpitude' for being accused of posting racist content on Twitter (BBC News 2019). There is also the aforementioned UK incident regarding Gareth Roberts and accusations of transphobic language. Such incidents imply general rules as to why morality clauses are put into author contracts and what kind of behaviour is not tolerated by publishers – in this case, problematic behaviour. In addition, documents such as 'An Industry-Wide Commitment to Professional Behaviour in Bookselling and Publishing' (Publishers Association 2018) from the Booksellers Association, Society of Authors, Publishers Association, and Association of Authors' Agents can be used to establish behavioural expectations for agents in the UK publishing field. Published in 2018, this code of conduct provides a formal account of what behaviour is considered unacceptable in the industry: '[The document] contains four principles, underpinned by a set of commitments to present a united vision for professionalism in the industry, to celebrate diversity and inclusion in all its forms, and to recognise the threats posed by abuse of power' (Publishers Association 2018).[32] While this document does not explicitly mention morality clauses, one of the principles states 'We will recognise our influence and make a commitment to work together to prevent abuse of power, creating a work environment free of discrimination, harassment including sexual harassment, bullying and intimidation' (Publishers Association 2018). Such statements depict the field's disruption due to a lack of tolerance concerning problematic behaviour, providing a degree of context in any dispute concerning an ambiguous morality clause. Should one accept a publishing agreement after this document was drafted, it stands that, as members of the publishing industry, these

---

[31] *Tynes* v. *Rare Bird Lit Inc,* Superior Court of the State of California, 6 June 2019, https://s3.documentcloud.org/documents/6143871/Natasha-Tynes-Complaint.pdf.

[32] At the time of writing, it was announced the report would be updated in 2023/2024 to 'better reflect the changes both in our industry, and in society' (Wood 2023).

behavioural standards now apply. While these principles are not enforce-able by law and are instead an industry code of practice, they are acknowl-edged by many agents in the industry. For example, Penguin Random House UK include the details of the document in their 'About Us' section on their website (Penguin Random House, n.d.). Ultimately, there are many examples in the industry highlighting a lack of tolerance for problematic behaviour to be drawn on for context should an ambiguous morality clause be contested (as explored in Chapter 1). It could therefore be argued that even ambiguously worded morality clauses can be inter-preted through the factual matrix, and such fears of abuse from ambiguous morality clauses are unwarranted. However, simultaneously there are additional reasons why an ambiguous morality clause might still be deemed unenforceable within a contract despite the aforementioned con-texts guiding morality clause interpretation. Taking the previous example, in *Tynes* v. *RareBird*,[33] the Tweets that triggered the publisher to cite 'moral turpitude' for the author's dismissal were produced during the duration of the publishing agreement, but with Roberts and Ebury, the Tweets were composed before the publishing agreement, and well before the 2019 publication date of the title in question. If an author had a morality clause that was ambiguous in its language that did not cite a timeframe, how could one draw from these contexts as to when the behaviour had to have taken place? As well as this, some authors are not removed from certain publishers' platforms when exhibiting problematic behaviour due to their positions in the field. LA07 expressed an awareness of these exceptions:

> I think a lot of publishers think they can get away with publish-ing very outrageous figures . . . Jordan Peterson, which – I've sat with people who work at Ebury and said like, 'don't you think this guy's terrible?' And they've gone 'yeah, but he makes us like twelve-million pounds a year' . . . I think some people

---

[33] *Tynes* v. *Rare Bird Lit Inc*, Superior Court of the State of California, 6 June 2019. https://s3.documentcloud.org/documents/6143871/Natasha-Tynes-Complaint.pdf.

> think that doing that is worth it to keep the publisher alive to be
> able to buy other books, finance other books.

As long as there exist exceptions to behavioural 'rules' concerning the
problematic, there will always exist doubt about the implied meaning of
an ambiguous morality clause.

The second morality clause collected for this Element bypasses some of
the aforementioned concerns about ambiguous morality clauses – both in
terms of ambiguous wording and in furthering the power imbalance between
author and publisher. The clause was utilised by a micro-publisher producing
a literary anthology and was active as of 2020 when it was provided for this
research. Morality Clause B reads as follows:

> The author also agrees to uphold the ethos of the press, and
> will not engage in homophobic, sexist, transphobic, whor-
> ephobic, racist, anti-semitic or Islamophobic behaviour or
> activities while published by [publisher]. If the author is
> found to be behaving in such a way to be contrary to
> [publisher's] ethos, the board will meet to discuss inclusion
> of the author's work in future reprints.

This clause presents a list of specific behaviours that go against the 'ethos'
of the publisher, offering specific parameters of behaviour they deem
unacceptable (in this case, behaviour considered problematic). One
could argue that this clause still does not go far enough in its specificity –
an author could believe their actions were not sexist, for example, while
the publisher could argue they *were* sexist due to the way the publisher
perceives the author's actions. Similarly, if using contextual information
to interpret the terms of the clause and drawing on Hoffman's first
and second principles of interpretation, the inclusion of 'transphobic'
may be interpreted differently by publisher and author due to widely
publicised debate within and beyond the publishing industry concerning
what constitutes this behaviour in the 2020s. Nevertheless, the inclusion
of specific behavioural terms provides more guidance as to what this
publisher considers unacceptable behaviour than a morality clause that
otherwise uses general, wide-reaching language.

When examining contractual clauses regarding an author's rights, Day (2023) contends that 'vague' terms can allow for 'later negotiation' (108), and argues that:

> the best way to tackle contract negotiations is for authors to be given the tools to help them understand publishing as a business and its attendant processes, to realise their work's true value in the market ... I believe this access to information can correct the power imbalance between authors and publishers and result in productive connections and communication with in-house staff. (156–157)

The morality clause's contents can be explicitly linked to various factors contributing to the perceived power imbalance between publisher and author, such as the relationship between author and publisher that exists within the contractual framework discussed in Section 3.1, and the shifting relationship between authors and readers resulting in new expectations of authors highlighted in Chapter 2. I agree with Day in that should authors be equipped with the correct 'tools' and information of the publishing process, they will be well-placed in contract negotiations and in the working relationship with their publisher overall. However, the complex nature of the morality clause, I argue, means that such tools are not enough in isolation. Concerning ambiguous morality clauses, Pinguelo and Cedrone (2009) note: 'given the constant state of flux in which "moral" behaviour is defined, it is rather difficult to discern a definition for "morality" or "moral behaviour" applicable in all circumstances' (352). In the case of Morality Clause B, whether or not a prospective author agrees with the publisher as to what they consider moral behaviour (and, if they disagree with these terms, they can walk away from this contract), the publisher has asserted their own stances and values; they do not rely on, for example, the interpretation of shifting 'public conventions and morals' as included in previous morality clause examples in this Element. This level of specificity, I argue, lessens the power imbalance between publisher and author – there is less room for the feared 'abuse' of the clause, as expressed by interviewees for this Element, wider industry discussion (for instance, the literary agent speaking to *Publishers Weekly* concerned about ambiguous clauses being utilised for financial benefits (Deahl 2018), and the Society of Authors (2017) expressing concern about clauses being 'impossibly wide'), and scholarship such as that from Sánchez Abril and Green (2017), who state that clauses giving contracting parties 'unlimited discretion to interpret broad, all-encompassing morals clauses' have the opportunity to terminate an 'economically disappointing relationship' under 'the pretence of moral objection' (42). Morality Clause B rejects observations that organisations will typically employ morality clauses with vague, ambiguous language to allow themselves 'extensive flexibility to terminate' an agreement which would provide the contracting party with protection and, ultimately, power in such an agreement (Pinguelo and Cedrone 2009, 370). And, finally, there is the unsettled status of the 'rules of the game' established by the field's changing habitus regarding author behaviour: for instance, discrepancies across the industry regarding behaviour that might end a contractual relationship for one author but not another. The morality clause itself is ultimately unsettled in its emergence in the publishing field and therefore, as Sánchez Abril and Green note (2017), when there is specificity in morality clause terms, 'there is a general interest in ensuring that parties have the ability to actually understand what it is they are agreeing to' (58).

The explicitly stated timeline specified by the press also lessens the power imbalance; the author's conduct will only be considered while published by the press. The publisher also lessens the power imbalance by proposing that the author's future with the publisher will be 'discussed' by the board: their work is not immediately withdrawn and the contract terminated (as was included in previous morality clause examples). The clause suggests the publisher is responsible for evaluating the behaviour as opposed to relying exclusively on audience reactions to the author's behaviour, and signifies who will discuss further action as opposed to the decision coming down to an undisclosed party who might make the decision 'behind closed doors', as it were. Of course, this morality clause will inherently protect the publisher from financial and reputational damage, but the definitions of unacceptable behaviour provided by the publisher leave less room for potential 'abuse' compared to a clause that is wide-reaching and contains ambiguous language. There is also something to be said for the size of the publishers and the morality clauses provided for this research. The two morality clauses utilised as examples in this chapter were provided by micro-publishers; as smaller organisations, they present less of a power imbalance between themselves and their contracted authors, compared to the imbalance large, conglomerate publishers may present.

4 Conclusion

This Element has presented an account of the changing habitus experienced by agents in the publishing field as a response to an increased focus on author behaviour. I contend that twenty-first-century social contexts have disrupted the publishing field; these social contexts have impacted the 'social expectations' (Roberts 2021) of readers, and have also manifested alongside the changing concepts of authorship, readership, and the changing author–reader relationship afforded by social media's emergence in the field. As established by scholars of literature and publishing studies (Johnson 2021, Kiernan 2021, Laing 2017, S. Murray 2018, Murray 2019, Thomas 2020), authors are increasingly expected to perform their role as an author and develop their brand on online platforms. This Element has delivered an evaluation of how the publishing field has been disrupted by authors' lives beyond the text becoming more visible than ever. 'Unreasonable' (Gulledge 2011, 44) conduct exhibited by authors beyond the text (and the subsequent response by publishers) can now impact an author's position in the field. Author interviewees in particular remarked on the role of social media when it comes to the scrutiny of their behaviour, reflecting on the changed relationship between author and readers in the twenty-first century. Author behaviour beyond the text, as a result, becomes a paratextual threshold. Readers can now engage with, or walk away from, texts depending on their views about the behaviour of the text's author. However, the termination of an author contract, whether via a morality clause or otherwise, can (at least temporarily) take this choice away from readers. The morality clause's emergence, and the increased focus on author behaviour, also reinforce the notion that author behaviour – particularly problematic behaviour – has the potential to impact their position in the field, as well as entry to the field in the first place.

Examining the emergence of the morality clause in practice, this Element has revealed issues with the clause's implementation both within and beyond the contract. The lack of agency authors felt over their own contractual terms spoke to an overarching power imbalance between author and publisher. This was further reinforced when authors and literary agents expressed a 'fear' of the morality clause and the potential ways it could be abused for financial gain and (in theory) a swift exit from a contractual agreement, particularly when the morality clause in question contains ambiguous language. The ambiguous language of some morality clauses also presented further issues with its implementation; such poor wording, as discussed in Chapter 3, could render the clause void should an author have the resources to challenge it. If this is the case, it can be an ineffective tool.

However, as discussed, industry findings on author earnings and income, as well as observations from interviewees, are indicative that many authors may not possess the resources to legally challenge such a morality clause. The morality clause's potential effectiveness when implemented with ambiguous language, then, stems from various shortfalls of the publishing industry; the lack of agency authors feel they have over their contracts, the 'take it or leave it' attitude felt by authors when it comes to signing publishing agreements, and the general lack of resources authors have to challenge such a contractual clause even if, in some instances, it is implemented ineffectively via ambiguous language that could be contested. The morality clauses collected for this research, offered by micro, independent publishers based in the UK, present solutions to some of these concerns. Their specificity leaves less room for doubt as to what kinds of behaviour are encompassed by the clause, and present fewer opportunities for the clause to be 'abused' (Deahl 2018) due to their lack of ambiguous language. My primary recommendations for the industry, should a morality clause indeed be included in publishing agreements, is implementing a non-ambiguous clause into author agreements. The implementation of a morality clause can be more beneficial to both parties (and should not the contract be beneficial to both?) when the language used is specific and the demands of the clause are communicated clearly. It would be naïve to suggest a clause such as the morality clause that has inherently conflicting interests between the contracting party and the talent could be devised to completely satisfy the demands of each.[34] But, in the interests of maintaining a productive and continued contractual relationship, concerns regarding a morality clause's ambiguity can at least be lessened should clear language be utilised on the part of the contracting party.

---

[34] Examining the morality clause in a US publishing context, Fulton (2023) makes the case for a 'reciprocal', two-way morality clause holding both publisher and author to account for their behaviour, which would also provide a more mutually beneficial solution to ambiguous morality clauses (213).

References

Albertalli, B. (@beckyalbertalli). (2018). Tweet, 2 April. https://x.com/beckyalbertalli/status/980839726071668736 (accessed 17 January 2024).

Ali, R. (2023). Why Diversity Tactics in the Creative Industries Continue to Fall Short. *The Conversation*, 31 March. https://bit.ly/3wxBEqN (accessed 15 January 2024).

Alter, A. (2018). Canceled Deals and Pulped Books, as the Publishing Industry Confronts Sexual Harassment. *New York Times*, 27 March. https://bit.ly/3V17MfW (accessed 15 January 2024).

Anthony, A. (2021). Philip Roth, Blake Bailey and Publishing in the Post-#MeToo Era. *The Guardian*, 27 June. https://bit.ly/3V4eYIg (accessed 15 January 2024).

Antonio Vargas, R. (2022). Blake Bailey, Biographer Accused of Harassment and Rape, to Publish Memoir. *The Guardian*, 27 July. https://bit.ly/4bUKg9X (accessed 18 January 2024).

Atiyah, P. S. (1996). *An Introduction to the Law of Contract*. New York: Oxford University Press.

Bakare, L. (2020). Julie Burchill's Publisher Cancels Book Contract over Islam Tweets. *The Guardian*, 15 December. https://bit.ly/3ysX8p8 (accessed 18 January 2024).

Barbas, S. (2016). *Movie Crazy: Stars, Fans, and the Cult of Celebrity*. Cham: Springer.

Barnett, D. (2020). Finally Working on That Novel as You Self-Isolate? You're Not Alone. *The Guardian*, 26 March. https://bit.ly/3X0gsEP (accessed 18 January 2024).

Bayley, S. (2022). Median Earnings for Authors Now Just £7,000, According to New Report from ALCS. *The Bookseller*, 6 December. https://bit.ly/3ysUqA0 (accessed 18 January 2024).

BBC News. (2017). Milo Yiannopoulos: Who is the Alt-Right Writer and Provocateur? 20 February. www.bbc.com/news/world-us-canada-39026870 (accessed 15 January 2024).

BBC News. (2019). US Author Loses Book Deal for Tweet-Shaming. 13 May. www.bbc.com/news/world-us-canada-48257825 (accessed 17 January 2024).

Belam, M. (2017). 'Unclear, Unfunny, Delete': Editor's Notes on Milo Yiannopoulos Book Revealed. *The Guardian*, 28 December. https://bit.ly/4akGqG2 (accessed 15 January 2024).

Blackshaw, I. (2003). It's Not Just Cricket! *Sport and the Law Journal* 11(3), 134–7. www.britishsportslaw.com/academic-2/ (accessed 5 June 2024).

Bland, A. (2021). Julie Burchill Agrees to Pay Ash Sarkar 'Substantial Damages' in Libel Case. *The Guardian*, 16 March. https://bit.ly/4dD0XZ9 (accessed 16 January 2024).

Blathwayt, R. (1892). A Talk with Dr. Conan Doyle. *The Bookman* 2(8), 50–1. www.arthur-conan-doyle.com/index.php/A_Talk_with_Dr._Conan_Doyle (accessed 30 May 2023).

Bond, P. 2016. Milo Yiannopoulos Strikes $250K Book Deal (Exclusive). *The Hollywood Reporter*, 29 December. https://bit.ly/4aoOAgi (accessed 15 January 2024).

Bourdieu, P. (1986). The Forms of Capital. J. G. Richardson ed., *Handbook of Theory and Research for the Sociology of Education*. Westport: Greenwood Press, pp. 214–58.

Bourdieu, P. (1990). *The Logic of Practice*. Stanford: Stanford University Press.

Bourdieu, P. (1993). *The Field of Cultural Production*. Cambridge: Polity Press.

Bourdieu, P. (1998). *Practical Reason*. Cambridge: Polity Press.

Bourdieu, P. (2010). *Distinction*. London: Routledge.

Brombley, K. (2017). A Case Study of Early British Sherlockian Fandom. *Transformative Works and Cultures* 23, n.p. https://doi.org/10.3983/twc.2017.0861.

Brook, O., O'Brien D., and Taylor, M. (2020). *Culture is Bad for You: Inequality in the Cultural and Creative Industries*. Manchester: Manchester University Press.

Bullen, C. (2022). 'Your Bookshelf is Problematic': Progressive and Problematic Publishing in the Age of COVID-19. C. Norrick-Rühl and S. Towheed, eds., *Bookshelves in the Age of the COVID-19 Pandemic*. Cham: Springer International Publishing, pp. 69–92.

Carlill v. *Carbolic Smoke Ball Co* [1893] 1 QB 256.

Carlsen, A., M. Salam, C. Cain Miller, D. Lu, A. Ngu, J. K. Patel, and Z. Wichter. (2018). #MeToo Brought Down 201 Powerful Men. Nearly Half of Their Replacements are Women. *New York Times*, 23 October. www.nytimes.com/interactive/2018/10/23/us/metoo-replacements .html (accessed 20 January 2024).

Chandler, M. (2019a). Diversity Warning as Full ALCS Author Earnings Survey Published. *The Bookseller*, 7 May. https://bit.ly/3VHB6bu (accessed 18 January 2024).

Chandler, M. (2019b). Ebury Drops Roberts from Doctor Who Book over Trans Tweets. *The Bookseller*, 5 June. https://bit.ly/3QKRkOn (accessed 18 January 2024).

Chandler, M. (2020). Publishers Cut Ties with David Starkey After 'Abhorrent' Comments. *The Bookseller*, 3 July. https://bit.ly/3WICGem (accessed 18 January 2024).

Chappell & Co Ltd v. *Nestlé Co Ltd* [1960] AC 97.

Chilton, L. (2020). Boycotting Hogwarts Legacy over J. K. Rowling Won't Achieve Much – But it's No Surprise Fans Are Considering it. *The Independent*, 19 September . https://bit.ly/3WItI0l (accessed 16 January 2024).

Clark, A. (2022). From Morality Clauses to Sensitivity Readers: Inside UK Publishing's Identity Crisis. *The New Statesman*, 16 July. https://bit.ly/ 3K3IZBw (accessed 15 January 2024).

Clayman Pye, V. (2022). Your Fave is Problematic: Anti-Fandom, Antefandom, and the Problem of Will. V. M. Fazel and L. Geddes, eds., *The Shakespeare Multiverse Fandom as Literary Praxis*. New York: Routledge, pp. 167–201.

Clifton, P. (2010). Teach Them to Fish: Empowering Authors to Market Themselves Online. *Publishing Research Quarterly* 26(2), 106–9. https://doi.org/10.1007/s12109-010-9160-9.

Conan Doyle, A. (1887). A Study in Scarlet. www.gutenberg.org/files/244/244-h/244-h.htm (accessed 30 May 2023).

Conan Doyle, A. (1893). The Final Problem. www.gutenberg.org/files/834/834-h/834-h.htm#chap12 (accessed 30 May 2023).

Cooley, H. A., M. B. Fleming, and G. McFadden-Wade. (2008). Morality and Money: Contractual Morals Clauses as Fiscal and Reputational Safeguards. *Journal of Legal Studies in Business* 14. https://bit.ly/3Vgrh2U (accessed 5 June 2024).

Cowdrey, K. (2020). Hachette Moves to Back Rowling after Staff Raise Concerns. *The Bookseller*, 16 June. https://bit.ly/3UPIKiC (accessed 16 January 2024).

Crawford, L. (2022). Why I'm Picking Trans Rights over Harry Potter. *British GQ*, 20 April. www.gq-magazine.co.uk/culture/article/harry-potter-trans-rights (accessed 17 January 2024).

Crockett, M. (2017). Roxane Gay Slams Publisher for Offering a Deal to Yiannopoulos. *Stylist*, 21 February. https://bit.ly/3yvzQz1 (accessed 18 January 2024).

Davidson, A. (2020). #MoralsToo: The Film Industry Must Implement an International Morals Clause. *Southwestern Journal of International Law* 26, 376. HeinOnline. https://bit.ly/3VH7ivO (accessed 5 June 2024).

Day, K. (2021). Publishing Agreements Through a Sharper Lens: How Relational Contract Theory Informs Author–Publisher Negotiations.

Publishing Research Quarterly 37(2), 152–167. https://doi:10.1007/s12109-021-09806-9.

Day, K. (2023). *Publishing Contracts and the Post Negotiation Space: Lifting the Lid on Publishing's Black Box of Aspirations, Laws and Money*. London: Routledge.

Deahl, R. (2018). In the #MeToo Moment, Publishers Turn to Morality Clauses. *Publishers Weekly*, 27 April. https://bit.ly/4554yLB (accessed 15 January 2024).

Denis-Smith, J. (2017). An Attack on the Past and a Guide to the Future? Lord Sumption's Latest Lecture. *Thomson Reuters*, 30 June. https://bit.ly/4b1octp (accessed 18 January 2024).

Dias v. *Archdiocese of Cincinatti*, 1:11-cv-00251 (S. D. Ohio 2011).

Dougan, M. B. (1977). 'A Touching Enigma': The Opera Career of Mary Lewis. *The Arkansas Historical Quarterly* 36(3), 258–279. https://doi.org/10.2307/40018535.

Dougan, M. B. (2018). Mary Sybil Kidd Maynard Lewis (1897–1941): 'I'm from the South and I've Got Plenty of Rhythm'. In C. Jones-Branch and G. T. Edwards, eds., *Arkansas Women: Their Lives and Times*. Georgia: University of Georgia Press, pp. 275–286.

Driscoll, B. (2021). How Goodreads is Changing Book Culture. *Kill Your Darlings*, 15 June. www.killyourdarlings.com.au/article/how-goodreads-is-changing-book-culture/ (accessed 17 January 2024).

Elgot, J. (2016). J. K. Rowling Condemns 'ugly' Rhetoric of EU Referendum Campaign. *The Guardian*, 20 June. www.theguardian.com/books/2016/jun/20/jk-rowling-eu-referendum-campaign (accessed 18 January 2024).

Epstein, C. (2015). Morals Clauses: Past, Present and Future. *New York University Journal of Intellectual Property and Entertainment* 5(1), 72–106. https://jipel.law.nyu.edu/vol-5-no-1-3-epstein/ (accessed 5 June 2024).

European Commission. n.d. SME definition. https://single-market-economy.ec.europa.eu/smes/sme-definition_en (accessed 1 August 2023).

Fallon, C. (2016). Critics Threaten Boycotts of Simon & Schuster Over Milo Yiannopoulos Book Deal. *HuffPost UK*, 30 December. https://bit.ly/3R8pagf (accessed 15 January 2024).

Fewery, J. (2021). Purpose Driven. *The Bookseller*, 11 March. www.thebookseller.com/comment/purpose-driven-1243715 (accessed 18 January 2024).

Flood, A. (2014). J. K. Rowling Presses the Case Against Scottish Independence. *The Guardian*, 8 September. https://bit.ly/4bR3uxL (accessed 18 January 2024).

Flood, A. (2018a). Junot Díaz Welcomed Back by Pulitzer Prize after Review into Sexual Misconduct Claims. *The Guardian*, 19 November. https://bit.ly/3V37VOy (accessed 15 January 2024).

Flood, A. (2018b). Three Women Go Public with Sherman Alexie Sexual Harassment Allegations. *The Guardian*, 7 March. https://bit.ly/3Km68z8 (accessed 15 January 2024).

Flood, A. (2020a). David Starkey Dropped by Publisher and University after Racist Remarks. *The Guardian*, 3 July. https://bit.ly/44YWv2Q (accessed 18 January 2024).

Flood, A. (2020b). Staff at Jordan Peterson's Publisher Protest New Book Plans. *The Guardian*, 25 November. https://bit.ly/3R37Hpw (accessed 16 January 2024).

Fulton, L. M. (2023). Frustrating Morals: Is There an Implied Reverse Morals Clause in Publishing Agreements? *Brooklyn Journal of Corporate, Financial & Commercial Law* (17)2, 206–228. htttps://brooklynworks.brooklaw.edu/bjcfcl/vol17/iss2/11 (accessed 5 June 2024).

Gallagher, M. S. (2016). Who's Really 'Winning'? The Tension of Morals Clauses in Film and Television. *Virginia Sports and Entertainment Law Journal* 16(1), 88–119. HeinOnline. https://bit.ly/3VFYDcJ (accessed 5 June 2024).

Gardiner, J. (2000). ''What is an Author?' Contemporary Publishing Discourse and the Author Figure. *Publishing Research Quarterly* (16), 63–75. https://doi.org/10.1007/s12109-000-1014-4.

Genette, G. (1997). *Paratexts: Thresholds of Interpretation*. Cambridge: Cambridge University Press.

Goldsmith, M. (2016). Exploring the Author–Reader Relationship in Contemporary Speculative Fiction: The Influence of Author Persona on Readers in the Era of the Online 'Author Platform.' *Logos* 27(1), 31–44. https://doi.org/10.1163/1878-4712-11112096.

Grady, C. (2017). Milo Yiannopoulos's Book Deal Represents a Troubling Shift in Conservative Publishing. *Vox*, 3 January. https://bit.ly/4bEFNbQ (accessed 15 January 2024).

Griswold, W., E. Lenaghan, and M. Naffziger. (2011). Readers as Audiences. In V. Nightingale ed., *The Handbook of Media Audiences*. New York: Wiley, pp. 17–40.

Griswold, W., T. McDonnell, and N. Wright. (2005). Reading and the Reading Class in the Twenty-First Century. *Annual Review of Sociology* 31 (1): 127–141. https://doi.org:10.1146/annurev.soc.31.041304.122312.

Gulledge, E. (2011). Understanding the Publishing Field: The Contributions of Bourdieu. Unpublished PhD disseration, University of St Andrews. http://hdl.handle.net/10023/3132 (accessed 5 June 2024).

Gulledge, E., P. Roscoe, and B. Townley. (2015). Economizing Habitus. *Journal of Cultural Economy* 8(6), 637–654. https://doi:10.1080/17530350.2015.1047785.

Harris, A. E. (2021). How Getting Canceled on Social Media Can Derail a Book Deal. *New York Times*, 11 February. www.nytimes.com/2021/02/11/books/morals-clause-book-deals-josh-hawley.html (accessed 5 June 2024).

Hay House. (2022). Manuscript Submission Deadlines. n.d. https://bit.ly/4b5jBGq (accessed 30 May 2023).

I. C. S. v. *West Bromwich Building Society* [1998] 1WLR 896 (HL).

Jamieson, A. 2017. Roxane Gay Pulls Book from Simon & Schuster over Milo Yiannopoulos Deal. *The Guardian*, January 25, 2017. https://bit.ly/4dYGyxO (accessed 15 January 2024).

Johnson, M. (2021). *Books and Social Media: How the Digital Age is Shaping the Printed Word*. London: Routledge.

Jones, H. and C. Benson. (2016). *Publishing Law, 5th Edition*. London: Routledge.

Jones, P. (2008). Random Defends Children's Clause. *The Bookseller*, 29 August. www.thebookseller.com/news/random-defends-childrens-clause (accessed 15 January 2024).

Jones, P. (2018). Rules for Scribes. *The Bookseller*, 15 June. www.thebookseller.com/comment/rules-scribes-808286 (accessed 16 January 2024).

Kaplan, L. (2021). My Year of Grief and Cancellation. *New York Times*, 25 February. www.nytimes.com/2021/02/25/style/your-fave-is-problematic-tumblr.html (accessed 15 January 2024).

Katz, S. D. (2011). Reputations – A Lifetime to Build, Seconds to Destroy: Maximizing the Mutually Protective Value of Morals Clauses in Talent Agreements. *Cardozo Journal of International and Comparative Law* 20, 185–232. HeinOnline. https://heinonline.org/HOL/P?h=hein.journals/cjic20&i=187 (accessed 5 June 2024).

Kiernan, A. (2021). *Writing Cultures and Literary Media: Publishing and Reception in the Digital Age*. Cham: Springer.

Koegler, C., C. Norrick-Rühl, P. Pohlmann, and G. Sieg. (2023). 'Must Writers Be Moral?': Interdisciplinary Perspectives on Morality Clauses in the Literary World. In E. Achermann, A. Blödorn, C. Norrick-Rühl, and P. Pohlmann, eds., *Literature and Law: Materiality*. *Literature and Law, vol. 1*. Berlin: J. B. Metzler, pp. 75–105.

Kressler, N. B. (2005). Using the Morals Clause in Talent Agreements: A Historical, Legal and Practical Guide. *Columbia Journal of Law & the Arts* 29, 235–260. HeinOnline. https://heinonline.org/HOL/P?h=hein.journals/cjla29&i=245 (accessed 5 June 2024).

Laing, A. (2017). Authors Using Social Media: Layers of Identity and the Online Author Community. *Publishing Research Quarterly* 33(3), 254–267. https://doi:10.1007/s12109-017-9524-5.

Lantagne, S. (2014). Sherlock Holmes and the Case of the Lucrative Fandom: Recognizing the Economic Power of Fanworks and Reimagining Fair Use in Copyright. *Michigan Telecommunications and Technology Law Review* 21, 263–315. https://doi.org/10.2139/ssrn.2402951.

Lawson, A. (2020). The UK's Reading Culture and Consumers' Emotional Response to Books. In A. Baverstock, R. Bradford. and M. Gonzalez, eds., *Contemporary Publishing and the Culture of Books*. London: Routledge, pp. 58–76.

Le Guin, U. K. (2011). Ursula K. Le Guin: A Blog. 18 January. https://bit.ly/4aHhBUC (accessed 18 January 2024).

Lebaron, F. (2014). Symbolic Capital. In A. C. Michalos ed., *Encyclopedia of Quality of Life and Well-Being Research*. Dordrecht: Springer Netherlands, pp. 6537–6543.

Leeds Times. (1893). A Great Detective. *Leeds Times*, 16 December 1893. British Library Newspapers. https://bit.ly/3RrhQww (accessed August 3, 2023).

Lewis, C. R. (2019). Very Online, When Authors Behave Badly on Twitter. *Bitch Media*, 22 November. https://web.archive.org/web/20220524062556/ https://www.bitchmedia.org/article/very-online-sarah-dessen-social-media-controversy (accessed 18 January 2024).

Lipton, D. J., (2020). *Law and Authors: A Legal Handbook for Writers*. California: University of California Press.

Little, M. (2011). Agenting Now. *Logos* (22)2, 22–27. https://doi.org/10.1163/095796511x580293.

Malkin, B. and Jacobs, B. (2017). Milo Yiannopoulos Disinvited from CPAC after Making Comments on Child Abuse. *The Guardian*, 20 February. https://bit.ly/4bRtWqg (accessed 15 January 2024).

Milo Yiannopoulous v. *Simon & Schuster Inc*, New York County Court, 7 July 2017. www.courthousenews.com/wp-content/uploads/2017/07/milo-yiannopoulos.pdf.

Mitchell, C. (2009). Contracts and Contract Law: Challenging the Distinction Between the 'Real' and 'Paper' Deal. *Oxford Journal of Legal Studies* 29(4), 675–704. https://doi:10.1093/ojls/gqp023.

Mitchell, C. (2022). *Vanishing Contract Law: Common Law in the Age of Contracts*. Cambridge: Cambridge University Press.

Morris, G. R. (2019). Media Moguls Risking It All: Contract Clauses in the Entertainment Business in the Age of #MeToo. *Arizona State University Sports and Entertainment Law Journal* 9(1), 1–47. HeinOnline. https://bit.ly/3VoBXN5 (accessed 5 June 2024).

Murray, J. (2018). Morality Clauses and Escrow Accounts in Sports Contracts. *Virginia Sports and Entertainment Law Journal* 17(2), 119–150.

Murray, S. (2018). *The Digital Literary Sphere: Reading, Writing, and Selling Books in the Internet Era*. Baltimore: Johns Hopkins University Press.

Murray, S. (2019). Authorship. In A. Philips and M. Bhaskar, eds., *The Oxford Handbook of Publishing*. Oxford: Oxford University Press, pp. 38–54.

Nader v. *ABC Television, Inc.*, 330 F. Supp. 2d 345 (S. D. N. Y. 2004).

Nash, R. (2013). What is the Business of Literature? *VQR*, 89, n.p. www.vqronline.org/articles/what-business-literature (accessed 5 June 2024).

New York Times. (1921). Morality Clause for Films: Universal Will Cancel Engagements of Actors Who Forfeit Respect. *New York Times*, 22 September.

New York Times. (1931). Mary Lewis Is Accused: Pathé Company say she Violated MoralsClause. *New York Times*, 25 February. https://bit.ly/4cniWS3 (accessed 5 June 2024).

Ng, A. (2009). The Social Contract and Authorship: Allocating Entitlements in the Copyright System. *Fordham Intellectual Property, Media & Entertainment*

Law Journal 19(2), 413–482. HeinOnline. https://bit.ly/3z2UEhP (accessed 5 June 2024).

Ng, E. (2020). No Grand Pronouncements Here . . . : Reflections on Cancel Culture and Digital Media Participation. *Television & New Media* 21(6), 621–627. https://doi.org/10.1177/1527476420918828.

North, A. (2017). More than 250 Powerful People Have Been Accused of Sexual Misconduct in the #MeToo Era. Here's a Running List. *Vox*, 22 December. www.vox.com/a/sexual-harassment-assault-allegations-list (accessed 15 January 2024).

Novelists Inc. 2010. Email newsletter to subscribers, November 2010, 21(11).

Nugent, A. (2020). Julie Burchill Book Contract Terminated by Hachette after Islamophobia Accusation. *The Independent*, 15 December. https://bit.ly/3KkSRqF (accessed 16 January 2024).

Nussbaum, E. (2014). Fan Friction. *The New Yorker*, 19 January, www.newyorker.com/magazine/2014/01/27/fan-friction (accessed May 30, 2023).

Osborn Hill, S. (2010). How to Protect Your Brand When Your Spokesperson Is Behaving Badly: Morals Clauses in Spokesperson Agreements. *The Federal Lawyer*, (January 2010). www.fedbar.org/wp-content/uploads/2010/01/ipinsight-jan10-pdf-1.pdf (accessed 5 June 2024).

Overdorf, M., and A. Barragree. (2001). The Impending Disruption of the Publishing Industry. *Publishing Research Quarterly* 17(3), 3–18. https://doi:10.1007/s12109-001-0027-y.

Owen, L. (2017). *Clark's Publishing Agreements: A Book of Precedents 10th Edition*. London: Bloomsbury.

Penguin Random House.(n.d). Industry Commitment to Professional Behaviour. www.penguin.co.uk/company/about-us/notices/professional-behaviour/ (accessed 18 January 2024).

Percival, A. (2018). J.K. Rowling Blames Liking Transphobic Tweet On 'Middle-Aged Moment'. *HuffPost UK* 25 March. https://bit.ly/3R8EDwP (accessed 18 January 2024).

Perrott, B. and L. Forsyth. (2018). And the Oscar Goes To . . . Freedom of Contract! *HFW*, March. www.hfw.com/And-the-Oscar-goes-to-Freedom-of-Contract-March-2018 (accessed 18 January 2024).

Phillips, A. (2019). Publishing and Corporate Social Responsibility. In A. Phillips and M. Bhaskar, eds., *The Oxford Handbook of Publishing*. Oxford: Oxford University Press, pp. 147–61.

Photo Production Ltd v. *Securicor Transport Ltd* [1980] AC 827.

Pinguelo, F. M. and D. T. Cedrone. (2009). Morals? Who Cares About Morals? An Examination of Morals Clauses in Talent Contracts and What Talent Needs to Know. *Seton Hall Journal of Sports & Entertainment Law* 19 (2), 347–80. https://scholarship.shu.edu/sports_entertainment/vol19/iss2/4 (accessed 5 June 2024).

Price, L. (2012). *How to Do Things with Books in Victorian Britain*. New Jersey: Princeton University Press.

Publishers Association. (2018) An Industry-Wide Commitment to Professional Behaviour in Bookselling and Publishing. https://bit.ly/4aJk2pM (accessed 18 January 2024).

Reardon Smith Line v. *Hansen-Tangen* [1976] 1 W.L.R. 989 (HL) [995-997].

Retirement Villages Developments Limited v. *Punch Partnerships (PTL) Limited* [2022] EWHC 65.

Roberts, N. (2021). Diversity and Inclusion in Publishing: What Do We Know? *Publishing Research Quarterly* 37(2), 255–263. https://doi:10.1007/s12109-021-09805-w.

Romano, A. (2020). Harry Potter and the Author Who Failed Us. *Vox*, 11 June. www.vox.com/culture/21285396/jk-rowling-transphobic-backlash-harry-potter (accessed 16 January 2024).

Romero, S., and A. M. Martínez Figueroa. (2021). 'The Unbearable Whiteness of Publishing' Revisited. *Publishers Weekly*, 29 January. https://bit.ly/4dXT4xC (accessed 18 January 2024).

Royle, J., L. Cooper, and R. Stockdale. (1999). The Use of Branding by Trade Publishers: An Investigation into Marketing the Book as a Brand Name Product. *Publishing Research Quarterly* 15(4), 3–13. https://doi:10.1007/s12109-999-0031-1.

Saha, A. and S. van Lente. (2022). Diversity, Media and Racial Capitalism: A Case Study on Publishing. *Ethnic and Racial Studies* 45(16), 216–236. https://doi:10.1080/01419870.2022.2032250.

Sánchez Abril, P. and Greene, N. (2017). *Contracting Correctness: A Rubric for Analyzing Morality Clauses. Washington and Lee Law Review* 74(1), 1–75. https://scholarlycommons.law.wlu.edu/wlulr/vol74/iss1/3 (accessed 5 June 2024).

Schmitz, M. (2015). Problematic. *The Hedgehog Review* 17(1), n.p. https://hedgehogreview.com/issues/too-much-information/articles/problematic (accessed 5 June 2024).

Schuessler, J. (2016). 'Post-Truth' Defeats 'Alt-Right' as Oxford's Word of the Year. *New York Times*, 15 November. https://bit.ly/3wVFxpE (accessed 15 January 2024).

Sheikha, J. (2019). Punishing Bad Actors: The Expansion of Morals Clauses in Hollywood Entertainment Contracts in the Wake of the #MeToo Movement. *Nova Law Review* 43(2), 203–233.

Shulevitz, J. (2019). Must Writers Be Moral? Their Contracts May Require It. *New York Times*, 4 January. www.nytimes.com/2019/01/04/opinion/sunday/metoo-new-yorker-conde-nast.html (accessed 15 January 2024).

Skains, R. L. (2010). The Shifting Author–Reader Dynamic: Online Novel Communities as a Bridge from Print to Digital Literature. *Convergence* 16 (1), 95–111. https://doi:10.1177/1354856509347713.

Skains, R. L. (2019). *Digital Authorship: Publishing in the Attention Economy*. Cambridge: Cambridge University Press.

Society of Authors. (2015a). CREATOR Fair Contract Terms. https://bit.ly/4bTidYo (accessed 18 January 2024).

Society of Authors. (2015b). SoA Calls for Action on Author Contracts. 8 July 2015. https://societyofauthors.org/News/News/2015/July/CREATOR-Launch (accessed 18 January 2024).

Society of Authors. (2017). Before You Sign Morality Clauses. July 15, 2017. https://bit.ly/4cnk48f (accessed 18 January 2024).

Somers, E. (2018). What Publishers' 'Morality Clauses' Actually Say, and how Agents are Reacting. *Publishers Lunch*, 5 September. https://bit.ly/3X06aUZ (accessed 15 January 2024).

Squires, C. (2007). *Marketing Literature: The Making of Contemporary Writing in Britain*. London: Palgrave Macmillan UK.

Squires, C. (2020). Sensing the Novel/Seeing the Book/Selling the Goods. In C. Norrick-Rühl and T. Lanzendörfer, eds., *The Novel as Network: Forms, Ideas, Commodities*. Cham: Springer International Publishing, pp. 251–270.

Squires, C. and P. Ray Murray. (2013). The Digital Publishing Communications Circuit. *Book 2.0* 3(1), 3–23. https://doi:10.1386/btwo.3.1.3_1.

Stefansky, E. (2016). Simon & Schuster Defend $250,000 Book Deal with 'Alt Right' Troll Milo Yiannopoulos. *Vanity Fair*, 31 December. www.vanityfair.com/news/2016/12/simon-schuster-defends-milo-book-deal (accessed 15 January 2024).

Thomas, B. (2020). *Literature and Social Media*. Abingdon: Routledge.

Thompson, B. J. (2012). *Merchants of Culture*. Cambridge: Polity Press.

Toliver, S. R. (2021). Critically Analyzing Black Female YA Speculative Fiction. In S. Witte, M. Gross, and D. Latham, eds., *From Text to Epitext: Expanding Students' Comprehension, Engagement, and Media Literacy*. Santa Barbara: ABC-CLIO, pp. 79–90.

Tynes v Rare Bird Lit Inc, Superior Court of the State of California, 6 June 2019. https://s3.documentcloud.org/documents/6143871/Natasha-Tynes-Complaint.pdf (accessed 5 June 2024).

UK Parliament. n.d. What is an Act of Parliament? www.parliament.uk/about/how/laws/acts/ (accessed 18 January 2024).

Ungure, E. and L. Gūtmane. (2020). 'It Is Often a Shot in the Dark': Power Relationship Dynamics in Book Publishing in Latvia, 1990–2017. *Logos* 31(1), 35–47. https://ssrn.com/abstract=4011742 (accessed 5 June 2024).

Velasco, J. C. (2020). You are Cancelled: Virtual Collective Consciousness and the Emergence of Cancel Culture as Ideological Purging. *Rupkatha Journal on Interdisciplinary Studies in Humanities Special Conference* (12)5, 1–7. https://doi.org/10.21659/rupkatha.v12n5.rioc1s21n2.

Vredenburg, J., S. Kapitan, A. Spry, and J. A. Kemper. (2020). Brands Taking a Stand: Authentic Brand Activism or Woke Washing? *Journal of Public Policy & Marketing* 39(4), 444–460. https://doi.org/10.1177/0743915620947359.

Weaver, M. (2015). Cambridge University Drops David Starkey Video after Racism Row. *The Guardian*, 19 November. https://bit.ly/3yFizDN (accessed 18 January 2024).

Williams, J. (2020). Hachette Workers Protest Woody Allen Book With a Walkout. *New York Times*, 5 March. www.nytimes.com/2020/03/05/books/hachette-woody-allen.html (accessed 16 January 2024).

Williams, J. B., L. Singh, and N. Mezey (2019). #MeToo as Catalyst: A Glimpse into 21st Century Activism Law in the Era of #MeToo. *University of Chicago Legal Forum* 2019, 371–394.

Wood, H. (2018). Morality Clauses 'Have Doubled' Over the Last Year. *The Bookseller*, 12 June. www.thebookseller.com/news/morality-clauses-have-doubled-over-last-year-802466 (accessed 18 January 2024).

Wood, H. (2023). Cross-Sector Body to Issue New Guidelines Against Harassment Five Years On. *The Bookseller*, 26 September.

https://www.thebookseller.com/news/cross-sector-body-to-issue-new-guidelines-against-harassment-five-years-on (accessed 18 January 2024).

Zarriello, A. (2015). A Call to the Bullpen: Alternatives to the Morality Clause as Endorsement Companies' Main Protection Against Athletic Scandal. *Boston College Law Review* 56(1), 389–431. https://papers.ssrn.com/sol3/papers.cfm?abstract_id=2457566.

Acknowledgements

I'd like to thank Professor Kim Barker for her invaluable insight and expertise in the area of contract law over the duration of my PhD. I also offer my thanks to Professor Claire Squires and Dr Adrian Hunter for their guidance, patience, and expertise.

Cambridge Elements ≡

Publishing and Book Culture

SERIES EDITOR
Samantha Rayner
University College London

Samantha Rayner is Professor of Publishing and Book Cultures at UCL. She is also Director of UCL's Centre for Publishing, co-Director of the Bloomsbury CHAPTER (Communication History, Authorship, Publishing, Textual Editing and Reading) and co-Chair of the Bookselling Research Network.

ASSOCIATE EDITOR
Leah Tether
University of Bristol

Leah Tether is Professor of Medieval Literature and Publishing at the University of Bristol. With an academic background in medieval French and English literature and a professional background in trade publishing, Leah has combined her expertise and developed an international research profile in book and publishing history from manuscript to digital.

ADVISORY BOARD

Simone Murray, Monash University

Claire Squires, University of Stirling

Andrew Nash, University of London

Leslie Howsam, Ryerson University

David Finkelstein, University of Edinburgh

Alexis Weedon, University of Bedfordshire

Alan Staton, Booksellers Association

Angus Phillips, Oxford International Centre for Publishing

Richard Fisher, Yale University Press

John Maxwell, Simon Fraser University

Shafquat Towheed, The Open University

Jen McCall, Emerald Publishing

ABOUT THE SERIES

This series aims to fill the demand for easily accessible, quality texts available for teaching and research in the diverse and dynamic fields of Publishing and Book Culture. Rigorously researched and peer-reviewed Elements will be published under themes, or 'Gatherings'. These Elements should be the first check point for researchers or students working on that area of publishing and book trade history and practice: we hope that, situated so logically at Cambridge University Press, where academic publishing in the UK began, it will develop to create an unrivalled space where these histories and practices can be investigated and preserved.

Cambridge Elements ⹀

Publishing and Book Culture

The Business of Publishing

Gathering Editor: Rachel Noorda

Dr. Rachel Noorda is the Director of Publishing at Portland
State University. Dr. Noorda is a researcher of
twenty-first-century book studies, particularly on topics of
entrepreneurship, marketing, small business, national identity,
and international publishing.

ELEMENTS IN THE GATHERING

A full series listing is available at: www.cambridge.org/EPBC

Printed in the United States
by Baker & Taylor Publisher Services